RADICAL DESIGN SOLUTIONS THAT BREAK THE RULES

RotoVision

A RotoVision Book

Published and distributed by RotoVision SA
Route Suisse 9
CH-1295 Mies
Switzerland

RotoVision SA
Sales and Editorial Office
Sheridan House, 114 Western Road
Hove BN3 1DD, UK

Tel: +44 (0)1273 72 72 68
Fax: +44 (0)1273 72 72 69
www.rotovision.com

10 9 8 7 6 5 4 3 2 1

ISBN: 978-2-88893-052-5

Art Director for RotoVision Tony Seddon
Design by Morris & Winrow
Cover design by Emily Portnoi
Typeset in ITC New Baskerville and Kievit

Reprographics in Singapore by ProVision Pte.
Tel: +65 6334 7720
Fax: +65 6334 7721

Printed in Singapore by Star Standard Industries Pte.

Contents

Once upon a time, everyone knew what a logo was meant to be: simple, constant, immediately recognizable, reproducible at different sizes, distinct, and easily readable. The logo, so it goes, stamps a unified image on products, stationery, or signage and ties them unambiguously to the company that issued them—in fact, the corporate logo's principle mission has for a long time been largely one of reassurance.

Its history has been well rehearsed and is intimately tied up with modernism. From Peter Behrens' development of the first "corporate identity" (as opposed to a mere logo) for German goods manufacturer AEG in 1907, to its apogee in the consumer boom following World War Two, it's a tradition that still sets a benchmark for many graphic designers. And American designer Paul Rand is probably still seen as the corporate logo's high priest; his logo designs for companies such as IBM, UPS, and ABC are still revered by designers the world over and always cited as "classical" examples of logo design.

For many it's a body of work that continues to underpin the unwritten rules of "good" logo design. They demonstrate graphic design alchemy that results in a fixed, simple, distinctive, precious, and commercially valuable product. But if you are a diehard fan of these logos, you might want to look away now because this book is about logo design that in one way or another sticks out its tongue and diverges from this canonical approach.

The world has changed, technologies are different, and not only have marketers' and designers' understanding of branding become infinitely more sophisticated, so also has that of consumers. While "classical" logos continue to be designed and can still be effective, alternative approaches are being increasingly explored. And it is not only large corporations that play the branding game—in a world saturated with marketing, individuals and tiny companies also have logos, even if it means availing themselves of logo design websites or software packages that promise a logo at the drop of a coin.

Logos can now appear anywhere—not just on business stationery or as an ideogram on soap packaging. As a consequence, the boundaries between branding and logo have been blurred. A logo has traditionally been seen as the visual essence of a brand, the source from which branding was seen to be derived, but this is no longer so clear. Packaging can now function as a mini advertising billboard rather than something that is merely stamped with a logo as a seal of assurance.

And as brands have proliferated and now have to compete in an increasingly noisy environment, achieving standout by doing the same things in terms of logos has become more and more difficult, which has led to designers, marketers, and brands experimenting with different, more unorthodox approaches to logo design.

Logo designs for the screen began to unravel one of the cardinal assumptions—that a logo should be as fixed and simple as the branding iron searing the flesh of a young steer. Instead logos, designers have realized, can be fluid, shifting, and "dynamic." But as has been noted, flexible logos predate the austere logo of modernism—take for instance, the Michelin Man, or Bibendum as he's also called. One of the most enduring of trademarks (introduced by the French tire manufacturer in 1898), it has always been implemented flexibly and Bibendum has been shown in a variety of guises.

This flexibility is becoming more prevalent. Take the comments of graphic designer Andrew Ashton of Studio Pip and Co., whose work is featured on pages 112–113, 126–127, and 158–159. Ashton says he has been "fixated with pushing the conventions of identity design" and asks: "In an age of

> *"Logos can be fluid, shifting, and dynamic"*

shifting media, why does a logo have to be one fixed mark? Why can't it be a shape, a variety of symbols, a color, a smell, a process, or a sound? I have worked on a range of brands and, while I developed rigorous style guides, I have been thinking of ways in which identities can be fluid, rather than fixed, and still communicate what modern clients require out of brands."

Of all the "rule-breaking" categories we feature in this book, logos that flout the convention of constancy are the most numerous. While flexibility within a logo design or brand architecture is one thing, completely changing a logo is another. Rebrands can be contentious—the acres of news coverage they often attract are not only due to outrage at the fees reportedly paid to the designers, but also a sign that people really care about the branding, be it for reasons of heritage, security, convenience, or whatever.

But the solemnity and totality of a logo is not what it once was. As another contributor to this book, Francheska Guerrero of Unfolding Terrain (see pages 57 and 132) notes, "the current life span of branding/identity programs is much shorter than the context in which the historical CBS logo was created. Today, in our hyper image-saturated subcultural markets, we continually seek the next 'fresh thing.' The universal audience no longer exists, we function in target demographics, and our logos—our identities—do not need to be watered down or become genericized trademarks for mass consumption."

Targeting younger consumers is harder and harder. While in the late 1980s and early 1990s corporate identities were briefly fashionable, the youth of today is more likely to have imbibed, even if at second or third hand, some of the arguments of Naomi Klein's seminal attack on the world of corporate brands in her best-selling book *No Logo*. They're able to "read" *Adbusters* and are as likely to engage with a noncorporate ID as with the highly selective (and ever changing) band of "acceptable" corporate (with a big C) identities.

"Technology has thrown the doors open for designers to experiment"

Creative strategies that would have been prohibitively complicated to implement have become relatively easy with the technology now available, throwing the doors open for designers to experiment. Of course, there are some sectors where experimentation is more prevalent than others. Many of the more daring logos that we feature in this book are for organizations such as galleries, public relations consultancies, music companies, or for designers themselves, where creativity is prioritized over the conventional and easy. While it may be more straightforward for companies and organizations such as these, particularly the smaller ones, to be experimental, they are also perhaps in the vanguard, pointing the way ahead. And while it is sometimes remarked that what is suitable for an art gallery might not be for a bank, that kind of thinking is also being loosened up.

Take the pastel-colored, soft-edged rebrand of British bank Abbey by Wolff Olins in 2003, which could indeed have been for a cultural institution. It shocked observers, and while it did not survive the bank's change of ownership in 2005, the branding showed the rules are there to be broken for all kinds of companies and organizations.

Indeed, Wolff Olins has tended to be pretty much alone among the large branding consultancies in devising identities that are visually challenging or which adopt innovative stances (its logos for Unilever and the New Museum in New York, for instance). It does not, at the time of writing, seem to have an identity itself, and has a tetchy relationship with the outside world, an approach no doubt born of the repeated outcry that its work has provoked. The biggest "logogate" of recent years followed the launch of Wolff Olins' unconventional logo design for the London 2012 Olympics. The media frenzy was intense and the scandal was international in its scope, with bloggers and commentators around the world heaping derision on the design. Permission to reproduce the logo in this book has not been granted, a sign of the continued sensitivity surrounding it.

"In the past, corporate identity was about control and consistency," said Karl Heiselman, Chief Executive of Wolff Olins, defending the work to *The New York Times*. "With too much control, what happens is that people forget about the content." Unfortunately this is something that Wolff Olins was unable to apply to itself. "We cannot be seen to be playing free and easy with our clients," Creative Director Martin Brown said to me while declining to participate in this book, perhaps in deference to the big ticket corporate clients that are the consultancy's bread and butter. It's a response that shows just how much is at stake when you break the rules with logo designs.

The frustration felt by many of the designers approached for this book was palpable—so often, when it comes to logo design, clients opt to play safe, consigning some of the more daring or unusual logo designs to the trashcan, never to see the light of day. We have included a few of these, as well as many instances where the designers were their own clients and able to give themselves free reign.

The traditional cookie-cutter approach to logo design and branding still works, but so increasingly do other approaches. Some of the innovations will no doubt become old hat, and seem of their time, but it is precisely this heightened ability we now have to read logos and date them, that means they are having to change more and more.

So in what follows, we have put together a collection of recent logo designs from around the world that dare to walk on the other side of the road. We have grouped them according to five principle logo misdemeanors. First, there are those that are difficult to read; second, those that break with expectation about what is appropriate for the company they are for; third, those that are fluid and changing, lacking in some way the constancy of a classical logo; fourth, those that shun simplicity, ease of reproduction, or ability to work at small sizes; and last, those that seem to incorporate mistakes of some sort. There is also a sin bin for other "rogues," or those unconventional logo designs that don't readily fall into the categories above.

Not every one of these logos is a masterpiece—though some are—but they show the different ways in which logo design is loosening up, exploring new avenues, and attempting to engage people anew. Now it's over to you.

Rule 1

CONVENTION HAS IT THAT ONE OF A LOGO'S FIRST TASKS IS TO BE IMMEDIATELY ACCESSIBLE AND READABLE; IT SHOULDN'T DAUNT THE VIEWER AT FIRST SIGHT. THE LOGOS THAT FOLLOW, HOWEVER, MAKE DEMANDS ON THEIR VIEWERS AND REQUIRE DECIPHERING.

THOU SHALT MAKE A LOGO THAT IS INSTANTLY READABLE

BIKINI WAX

DESIGN AND ART DIRECTION

Chris Bolton

RULE 1... AND HOW TO BREAK IT!

You don't always want people to be able to understand your logo too quickly. A tease can sometimes be much more effective.

We Got Beef is a bar-cum-nightclub in the Finnish capital Helsinki; Bikini Wax was a regular club night held at the venue, specializing in playing softer sounds such as bossa nova and soul. Chris Bolton was asked to come up with "a logo or image that would express the name in a dynamic way." Obviously, too literal an approach was out of the question, so Bolton played around with various associative elements inherent in the name. He came up with the idea of setting the name in a compact sans-serif font, partly covered by hair. "All the elements work together to create a solid image that could be considered more an illustration than a classic logo. Illustrative forms overlap and work inside and out of the words 'bikini wax,' adding a sense of dimension and movement to the logo," explains Bolton. Making the words difficult to discern only added to the effect of the slightly risqué name of the club night. The logo, perhaps because of its illustrative nature, was well received and was used for a variety of applications, including T-shirts.

FEEDBACK

"They liked it enough to make posters, T-shirts, and even a series of buttons using the logo."

CHRIS BOLTON

Bikini Wax
DJ Mary Mary & DJ Aleks Duplee
We Got Beef, Iso Roobertinkatu 21, Hki
Perjantai 🔲🔲.🔲🔲

How Do You Look?

DESIGN *Christian Küsters,*
CHK Design

RULE 1... AND HOW TO BREAK IT!
Remaining true to your subject
can mean carte blanche to ignore
the normal assumptions about
what a logo should be.

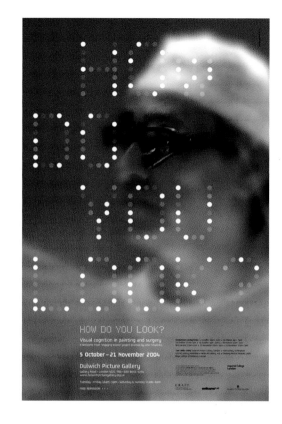

For most people a logo is something that should be noticeable rather than almost imperceptible. But this is a logo for an exhibition looking at the human eye and the mechanisms of visual perception, so something a little daring was appropriate. *How Do You Look?* was a traveling exhibition organized by the University of the Arts London, Imperial College London, and the Wellcome Trust. Designer Christian Küsters got right into the science involved. "The logo of the exhibition directly reflects the eye-tracker biomedical tool, which was used as part of the exhibition's research," he explains. "The eye-tracker is used extensively in psychology and visual studies, it records fixations, saccades, and gaze paths. This science of looking directly affected the identity. The final logo design is constructed to function as a strong identity and visually displays how the viewer looks at it; the connecting red lines mirror saccades and their consequent fixations and gaze paths."

Boutique London

DESIGN *SEA Design*

Boutique London is an annual fashion event held at the Earls Court exhibition center. The event organizers asked London-based SEA Design to develop a logo that would suggest both elegance and creativity. The logo design SEA developed has the words "boutique" and "London" cut in such a way as to be letters randomly fitting a shape that approximates the letter "B," sometimes even being cropped quite radically. A number of lock-ups and colors were then developed of the logo, which was intended to work with a variety of media.

RULE 1... AND HOW TO BREAK IT!
Rather than describing an event, let the logo's various forms embody its values.

MUDAM (MUSÉE D'ART MODERNE GRAND-DUC JEAN)

DESIGN *Ott+Stein with Oliver Peters*

Mudam is a museum of modern art with a difference—all aspects, from the architecture, to the café, to the graphics, are conceived as being part of the art, as a kind of design "Gesamtkunstwerk" in continual evolution. Look at its logo, a strange vertical series of marks, and it takes some time to decipher what language and alphabet are being used, let alone what the marks describe. The logo was designed by Berlin-based graphic design studio Ott+Stein, working together with Oliver Peters, who developed the remarkable typography inspired by the characters of written Japanese. The marks that make out the letters of Mudam only very loosely correspond to the Roman alphabet. This abstruseness is relished by the museum, which proudly announces that "these strange yet familiar new signs are accurate metaphors for Mudam's approach and go against established codes by giving rise to a liberating cognitive effort."

RULE 1... AND HOW TO BREAK IT!
Let people know about your intellectual ambitions by making them use their minds even when trying to decipher your logo.

FLOATING HEAVY

DESIGN *Stephen Heath, Red Design*

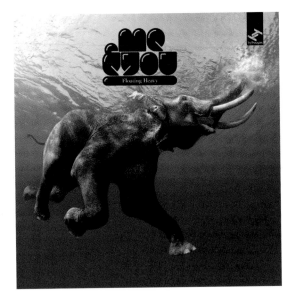

Floating Heavy

RULE 1... AND HOW TO BREAK IT!
Pulling the viewer in doesn't always
mean making it easy on him or her.
And here the difficulty is thematically
linked with the subject in hand.

Floating Heavy was the title of the debut album by TM Juke and Robert Luis, the duo who make up Me&You. An eclectic and mainly instrumental trawl through different genres, from jazz to breakbeat, the album was released by the Tru Thoughts record label. For the bespoke logotype and alphabet, Stephen Heath at Red Design developed some "extremely heavy, highlighted letterforms" intended to encapsulate the feeling of the album's title, a heaviness matched by the image of the swimming elephant. While the photograph was easy to read, if not immediately decipherable at first glance, the logo certainly wasn't.

"First we created the basic letterforms that would make up the alphabet, and then with some fine-tuning we created the logo. It purposefully pushes legibility and makes the viewer work harder than usual to 'decode,'" says Heath.

✝

F E E D B A C K
*Initially the client was cautious, but after living with
the design for a day or two they became convinced that it
was the right solution. But according to a BBC reviewer
it was a "stinking sleeve."*

FOSTER McGINTY

DESIGN *Jesse Kuhn,*
RAWTOASTDESIGN

Jesse Kuhn is a New York–based designer and illustrator, who was asked to come up with a logo for Foster McGinty, a band whose music Kuhn describes as a "raw combination of colorful riffs draped over funky grooves." His design, which needed to be representative of the band, sticks to these qualities of overlapping and rawness. While difficult to read at first, swirling around as it does, it is much easier to unpick for fans, who Kuhn says would identify the "hypnotic twists of circus showmanship" with the qualities that are at the heart of the band. "The circus rockabilly fashion sense and a red, white, and black palette is something fans connect with the band because of a very distinctive jacket the lead singer commonly wears," he explains.

RULE 1... AND HOW TO BREAK IT!
Not everyone needs to be able to read a logo, particularly if the subject has a cult following of fans who will pick up on visual clues.

G13 ART GALLERY

DESIGN *David Barath*

RULE 1... AND HOW TO BREAK IT!
Remaining appropriate to the ethos
of the gallery meant challenging
the viewer rather than making
things simple.

Taking its name from its address at 13 Gozsdu Court in the Hungarian capital Budapest, the G13 Art Gallery specializes in showing classic modernist works by famous Hungarian artists such as László Moholy-Nagy and André Kertész, alongside contemporary pieces. The space it occupies is, according to designer David Barath, "brutal and very industrial," and this was something he wanted to reflect in the logo he created for the G13. As well as being industrial, the mark also had to capture "a very austere, angular, and rough style" to reflect the uncompromising nature of the art shown by the gallery.

The logo pares down the name as much as is possible, challenging the viewer, much as the exhibited art does, to make sense of its visual strategy. "I have simplified the name until it cannot be simplified further—if you take just one simple element away, it makes no more sense," says Barath. "It is still legible, but looks like a constructivist piece of art itself."

✣

F E E D B A C K
"The logo exemplifies modern design and simplicity while being both elegant and professional. It is different and memorable at the same time."

FRANCISKA BRAY-MEZEY, DIRECTOR OF G13 ART GALLERY

Lost in Adaptation, SWISH

DESIGN *Jonny Costello, Fluid Design*

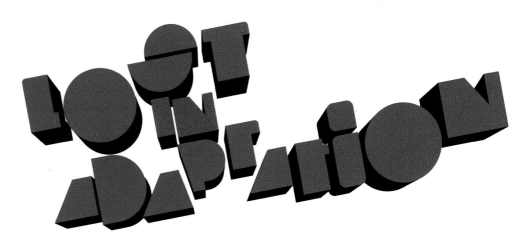

RULE 1... AND HOW TO BREAK IT!
Unusually in this case a lack of legibility was part and parcel of what the logo needed to impart, and the fact that the type forms had clearly been "pushed" was totally appropriate, despite the loss of immediate clarity.

Many movies have their origins in novels, and the relationship of one to the other was the subject of a film festival staged in Birmingham, UK, by creative consultancy, SWISH. The festival's title, Lost in Adaptation, begs the question of this relationship while playing on the title of Sofia Coppola's very successful movie *Lost in Translation*. As the theme was all about how something copes with the transition from one medium to another, Jonny Costello decided to develop a logo that would be "abstracted" from an absent originary logotype. So a simple starting point of a basic sans-serif typeface was "subjected to a process of simplification and abstraction into basic geometrical shapes," says Costello.

The lack of clarity and legibility of the final logo went to the heart of what the festival was all about.

Scale Architecture

LOGO DESIGN *Karlee Bannon*
COLLATERAL TYPOGRAPHY *Dan Ellis,
Wishart Design*

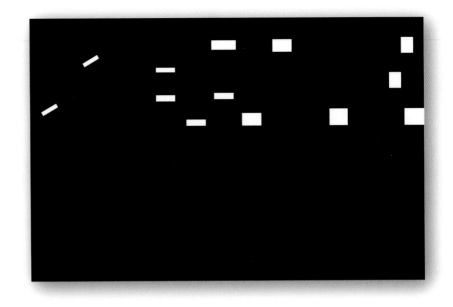

RULE 1... AND HOW TO BREAK IT!
What is readable here is not a word,
but a willingness to take risks and
engage the viewer intellectually.

L 6/2-12 FOVEAUX ST, SURRY HILLS. NSW 2010 AU
T: +61.2 9280 2180 F: +61.2 9280 2181
E: INFO@SCALEARCHITECTURE.COM

SCALE ARCHITECTURE

MATTHEW CHAN 0424 093 310

It takes a detailed explanation to realize that the minimalist hieroglyphics that make up the logo for Scale Architecture actually spell out the word "scale." But Scale Architecture, a design studio for architecture and urbanism, was keen that its logo should be experimental. The brief to fellow Sydney-based practice Wishart Design stipulated that the logo should be sophisticated and abstract yet versatile enough to be used in all its communications.

"This job was exciting because the client early on was willing for us to push boundaries," says Karlee Bannon. "This freedom and trust encouraged exploration of the identity and experimentation with the word 'scale.' The end result was rewarding in that the identity encouraged thought and a degree of deciphering to appreciate what was beneath the graphic."

While the blocks making up the logo seem like houses drawn to a small scale on an architect's plan, they were in fact the result of experimentation with the word "scale," with blocks placed over the areas of the letters which were then removed to leave the logo design. Type itself plays no part in the final logo.

TCO
(THE CONSCIENCE
ORGANISATION)

LOGO DESIGN *Karlee Bannon,*
Wishart Design

RULE 1... AND HOW TO BREAK IT!
Recognition offers a different kind
of readability to being simply able to
discern letters, and one probably more
appropriate for a company that prides
itself on being unconventional.

TCO is an Australian digital and broadcast branding agency that prides itself
on taking a creative and unconventional approach to its clients' needs. It
approached Wishart Design to come up with a refreshed and consolidated
visual identity that it could use in all its communications. While being
quirky and fun, it would have to be a solution that would be adaptable in
the future and work effectively in all media including digital and animated
screen environments, as they form the consultancy's mainstay. "The result
is a logo that is not easy to read, yet is instantly identifiable as TCO," says
Karlee Bannon at Wishart Design. "With TCO being a predominantly
screen-based company, the logo evolved through various experimentations
with pixels, which inspired the blocking in the letters."

A secondary logo was created along similar vibrant, pseudo-pixelated
lines to embody the company slogan "spread the love," which TCO uses to
both describe its relationship to its clients and for its charitable work. "The
director's business cards were printed half-and-half to establish the brand
among clients at random. The treatment of the main logo is such that it
can be abstracted and applied across a variety of media," adds Bannon.

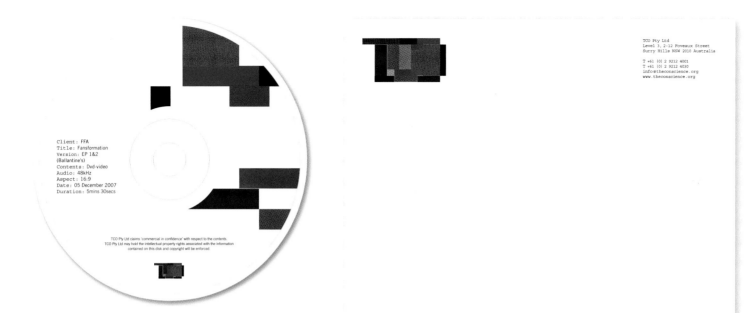

Client: FFA
Title: Fansformation
Version: EP 1&2
(Ballantine's)
Contents: Dvd-video
Audio: 48kHz
Aspect: 16:9
Date: 05 December 2007
Duration: 5mins 30secs

TCO Pty Ltd claims 'commercial in confidence' with respect to the contents.
TCO Pty Ltd may hold the intellectual property rights associated with the information
contained on this disk and copyright will be enforced.

TCO Pty Ltd
Level 3, 2-12 Foveaux Street
Surry Hills NSW 2010 Australia

T +61 (0) 2 9212 4001
T +61 (0) 2 9212 4030
info@theconscience.org
www.theconscience.org

ABN 69 125 933 637 | TCO Pty Ltd claims 'commercial in confidence' with respect to the contents.

✝

FEEDBACK

"It represents the versatility of TCO as a team and the constant possibilities that we can create in every job we do… it allows greater freedom in how we present ourselves."

TCO TEAM

✝

FEEDBACK

"The logo is not obvious and makes people and brand managers think in this blatant and obvious world."

CLIVE BURCHAM, TCO FOUNDER AND DIRECTOR

Yahoo! Games

design *Ian Lynam*

RULE 1... AND HOW TO BREAK IT!
Being legible is tantamount to politeness, and as the whole idea here was to suggest uncouth bad manners, that went out the window.

E3 Expo is a flagship convention for the electronic gaming industry, and Yahoo! Games wanted its presence to be felt. So it asked Ian Lynam, an American designer based in Tokyo, to come up with a series of heavy metal inspired logos for its different games, all with the intention of making the games seem "badass," says Lynam. The only stipulation was that these sublogos would have to take an original twist on the existing branding.

Lynam's enthusiastic response was a series of logos that pushed attitude over legibility—the fact that you had to work hard to decipher the games they referred to only added to the desired effect. The logos were used for banners at the convention, as well as various forms of promotional apparel.

Mɴ

DESIGN *Chris Trivizas*

RULE 1... AND HOW TO BREAK IT!
The logo effectively communicates the subjects of hair and femininity, which is perhaps more pertinent than making the actual initials legible.

✝

F E E D B A C K
"Unique and fresh, and instantly understandable as it points to hairdressing."
MARIA NAIKA

Taking its inspiration from a 1970s hairstyle, this swirly, humorous logo was created for a hairdressing salon on the Greek island of Corfu. If you can look past the hair, you will note that the logo is actually made up of the initials of the salon's owner—Maria Niaka. "The salon is a contemporary, pleasant, cosy place, in which pink and purple dominate, creating a warm, friendly, and very feminine atmosphere," explains Chris Trivizas, the Athens-based designer who devised the logo. "The aim was to design a logo that reflects the character of the salon, while also attracting custom." The choice of purple picks up on the color scheme of the salon as well as enforcing the 1970s reference.

NOTEWORTHY

DESIGN *Gregory Paone,*
Paone Design Associates

RULE 1... AND HOW TO BREAK IT!
With a finely attuned audience such
as this, taking a cryptic and puzzle-like
approach is more likely to draw them in
than push them away.

The Philadelphia Youth Orchestra produces a newsletter with the punning title of *Noteworthy*. Designing its masthead/logo, Gregory Paone decided to merge actual musical notation with custom letterform design to create something that is slightly cryptic yet playful and rhythmic. "The identity was the result of a sketch process which explored musical notation and symbols," explains Paone. "The playful yet sophisticated combination of forms alludes to music—the core mission of the organization. Its puzzle-like quality provides a 'discovery point' for the user while increasing brand awareness." While its form may be complicated, the simple print process of the newsletter meant it had to work in a single color.

FEEDBACK

"Musicians in the audience were well equipped to decipher the 'code' of the forms. Others enjoyed the point of discovery after receiving more than one issue of the newsletter. Knowing full well the repeated exposure would slowly introduce the masthead, the mark was not compromised in the design phase."

GREGORY PAONE, PAONE DESIGN ASSOCIATES

EYE PETROL

DESIGN *Jorge Aragon/Jork,*
Mediawork

RULE 1... AND HOW TO BREAK IT!
Online legibility becomes less of
an issue if the name is printed in
the URL, allowing the boundaries
of legibility, theoretically at least,
to be pushed further.

Eye Petrol is an online design magazine "run by its contributors," and one
of its first moves was to have an open competition for a logo and branding
design. Jorge Aragon, or Jork, a designer based in Buenos Aires, Argentina,
submitted these three challenging logos. Pushing legibility to its very limit,
they also managed to fall foul of the judges, who opted in the end for a
safer design.

FEMININE

DESIGN *André Nossek, Via Grafik*

RULE 1… AND HOW TO BREAK IT!
Hidden away in this logo are some details, such as the allusion to breasts, which require the camouflage of a complicated logo that needs slow deciphering rather than instant consumption.

Secret Lingerie is a Netherlands-based manufacturer of erotic clothing for women. For a promotional event in Spain, Secret Lingerie asked German graphic designers Via Grafik to come up with a logo that could be used for posters, allowing them to interpret "femininity" in their own terms rather than in the standard idiom of lingerie products, with their pastel colors and predictable swooshes. The resultant logo is suggestive and sensual in various unconventional ways, while remaining just about decipherable.

Human Magazine

design *André Nossek, Via Grafik*

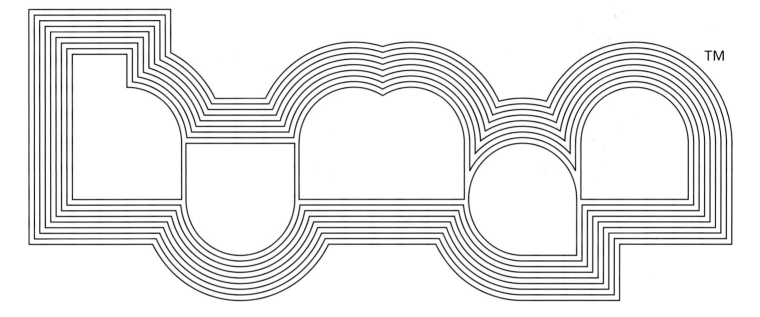

TM

RULE 1... AND HOW TO BREAK IT!
A logo doesn't necessarily need to be legible to be distinctive.

Conventional wisdom has it that magazine logos or mastheads should shout from the newsstand. In a sea of titles, the idea is they should be bold and fight for attention with neighboring titles with strong, instantly legible logos that can be spotted from a distance. But André Nossek, at Wiesbaden, Germany-based Via Grafik decided to do something different for a magazine called *Human*: "We wanted to break away from the normal magazine logos and came up with a very fragile version based on a very heavy font."

Medraw

DESIGN *Lars Herzig, Via Grafik*

RULE 1... AND HOW TO BREAK IT!
The attitude of the logo is instantly discernible even if the name isn't.

ETF Textil is a large manufacturer of T-shirts. It wanted to establish a new label, Medraw, and approached German graphic designers Via Grafik to come up with a name and logo. The result was an angry childlike scrawl, which is eventually decipherable as Medraw, the grammatical awkwardness echoing the provocation of the logo.

ALPHABET SOUP

ART DIRECTION *Brendan Elliott*
DESIGN *Terry Ricardo*
B&Co.

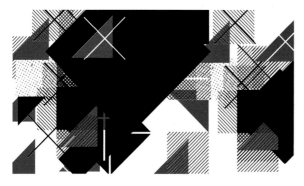

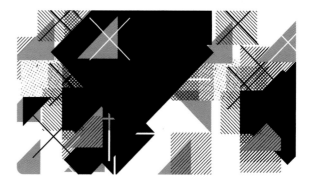

RULE 1... AND HOW TO BREAK IT!
Visual pleasure rather than instant legibility is more likely to get the target audience—children—on side.

Children's clothing company Alphabet Soup needed an identity and the only stipulation was that it needed to be adaptable and have the ability to evolve. Given the typographic mayhem suggested in the name, the designers at Melbourne-based agency B&Co. decided to have a bit of fun. The unorthodox, and not especially reader friendly, typography seems to be made up of art deco letterforms that have been "filled in." These are juxtaposed with a busy patterning to further confuse and/or intrigue the eye.

LEVI'S BLUE

DESIGN AND ART DIRECTION
Chris Bolton

RULE 1... AND HOW TO BREAK IT!
Make the viewer work to understand what he or she is reading and you will draw them into your world, while making it clear that this isn't your normal, everyday logo for an everyday product.

Levi's Blue is a premium line of clothing, produced by the legendary jeans brand. Chris Bolton was asked to design the visuals for the opening night of a Levi's Blue pop-up store in Antwerp, Belgium. Inspired by the Nu Rave theme of the event, Bolton, a British/Canadian designer based in Finland, came up with a solution that pushes the boundaries of legibility. He describes it as follows: "Horizontal lines create structured letterforms. When the words 'pop' and 'store' are used together, the word 'up' drops into the combination to create a readable, structured logo."

It is a multilayered design that Bolton admits is "more a strong graphic, typographic solution than a classic logo." No doubt its experimental feel was ideal for differentiating the Blue clothing line from Levi's standard fare. And it certainly put clear blue water between itself and the iconic, and very legible, primary Levi's logo. While initially intended for a single event, the logo was so well received that it has since been adapted and developed for all the communications of Levi's Blue.

LEVI'S® BLUE POP UP STORE
    LAUNCH PARTY
    20/03/2008
    21H·00 - 02H·00
–
In Collaboration With:
    CLINIC
    DE BURBURESTRAAT 5
    ANTWERPEN - SOUTH
–

EXCLUSIVE LIVE CONCERT
    22H·00
    FANCLUB DJ'S
–
LEVI'S® BLUE POP UP STORE
    OPEN FROM:
    21/03-21/05/2008
–
    WWW.LEVIS.BE
–

✝

FEEDBACK

*Though initially developed for the
opening of a single store, the identity
was adopted for all the visuals for the
premium Levi's Blue line.*

GOLDIEROCKS

ART DIRECTION *Ross Stirling and Dom Williams*
DESIGN *Ross Stirling*
Studio Juice

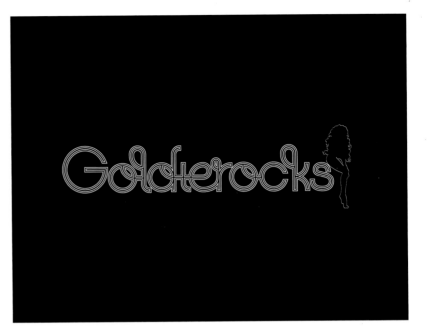

RULE 1... AND HOW TO BREAK IT!
Period style and allusion takes precedence over legibility for this personal identity.

Goldierocks is the nom de plum of Sam Hall, a UK-based DJ and journalist, who presents herself as a "blonde-haired vixen and rock 'n' roll talent spotter de jour." Her pseudonym is a reference to her distinctive heavy head of long blonde locks, a feature that was taken up by Studio Juice in its design for her personal identity. She wanted something that would be both feminine and retro. The logo presents her name as if it were a neon sign, but uses a custom font. "To avoid the cliché of a neon sign, we created a bespoke typography that feels retro," says Studio Juice's Ross Stirling. The client herself makes a cameo appearance in silhouette perched on the end of the logotype. The intricate, complicated forms of the custom typeface are a further reference to Goldierocks' trademark hair.

BRIK

ART DIRECTION *Rob Coke*
DESIGN *Stewart McMillan*
Studio Output

·RULE 1... AND HOW TO BREAK IT!
When the overall shape and support logo are clear, the main logotype can be a bit more challenging, especially for a one-off business such as this.

Brik is a barbershop in the center of the city of Nottingham in the UK. Its owners approached local graphic design group Studio Output looking for a logo that would be modern, yet also express the classic, art deco–inspired interior of the salon. The resultant logo merges both 1930s and contemporary looks to create a logo that prioritizes style over legibility, which is unusual for a barbershop.

FEEDBACK
"The lozenge style of the logo is instantly eye-catching on signage, flyers, and posters, and business is doing well."
BRIK

CORPORATE IDENTITY INSTITUTE

DESIGN *Robert Paulmann*

RULE 1... AND HOW TO BREAK IT!

Designing a logo about logos is tricky, but by making it hard to read people are encouraged to think about the function of a logo.

In 2008, Robert Paulmann set up the Corporate Identity Institute, an online presence that is aligned to the Design Faculty of the University of Applied Sciences in Mainz, Germany. It seeks to combine an academic approach with a forum for professional designers and businesses. While the logos that are its subject matter can range from the most classic and simple to the most rule breaking and radical, the Institute's own logotype seems smudged, as if printed incorrectly, even though it is designed for online use. "We tried to visualize the different aspects and complexities of corporate identities by using layers, which indicate the multiple levels and on the other hand create new and unpredictable figures within the logo itself," explains Paulmann.

Re:Creation (National Creativity Awards)

ART DIRECTION *Paul West*
DESIGN *Paul West and Nick Hard*
Form

UK fashion and culture magazine *Dazed & Confused* teamed up with youth fashion retailer Topshop to create an awards program and an accompanying traveling exhibition of fashion, journalism, photography, and art. Parties in six different cities with DJs and bands helped build the project's profile, as did the graphics designed by Form, who were responsible for the logo and all related event material including posters, adverts, invites, and flyers. The logo's intensely decorative nature meant legibility was pushed into the background, as the viewer tried to work out the name and punctuation in negative space.

RULE 1... AND HOW TO BREAK IT!
Let people have some visual pleasure before they do the hard work of deciphering what it is all about.

Cimex Usability Lab

DESIGN *Design Friendship*

RULE 1... AND HOW TO BREAK IT!
When confusion and discernibility are
the subjects at hand, why not exemplify
them in the logo?

As boundaries become blurred, it is sometimes not easy to say whether a piece of design is a logo, illustration, or advertisement. Take, for instance, the graphic Design Friendship was asked to create for the window of Cimex, a digital agency based in London, to "grab the attention of passersby and inform them of their Usability Lab." The lab uses eye-tracking technology to test user responses to websites, and this formed the basis of the illustrative design, underneath whose complex forms the word usability is ultimately discernible. "As the design process kicked in, the window graphic manifested into a logo for the lab, which represented an emotional journey that a web user would go through when visiting a website in an internet web browser window," explain the designers.

ESPIONAGE

ART DIRECTION *Patrick Duffy*
DESIGN *Patrick Fry*
Espionage

RULE 1... AND HOW TO BREAK IT!
Why not slice a bit off and share your logo with your clients; the audience is clever enough to get it.

Espionage is a multidisciplinary branding agency, whose logo has a "split personality" that appears on all the company's stationery and its website. Cut at an angle, the logo seems to partly hide on the page much as a spy might hide behind a tree. Designed to work on its own, the Espionage logo can also be completed by the inclusion of an extra word, be it a department or client's name, which instantly personalizes all correspondence. The "full word" logo has also been shortened to just an "E," which is animated as a splash page on the website. From one small E, there's now a gallery of siblings, happily fragmenting in a variety of different ways.

GET

DESIGN *Eirik Seu Stokkmo,*
Scandinavian Design Group

Get is one of Norway's major cable and broadband suppliers, and wanted to rebrand to consolidate its position. The ubiquity of the word "get" was one of the principle issues for designer Eirik Seu Stokkmo of Oslo-based Scandinavian Design Group. "A more distinct logo that would intrigue seemed like a wise decision to make sure the logo became a brand and not just a word," he says. "The flow and the shape, and other associations, became more important than legibility, when we realized this would make a stronger impact and create a presence that would be remembered. The characteristic initial 'G' caused a great deal of concern at the [early design] meetings, but has proven to be one of the logo's main assets."

RULE 1… AND HOW TO BREAK IT!
By creating a curious shape for the initial G, not only does the logo become a brand rather than a word, but it also offers a distinctive property that can be used on its own.

F E E D B A C K
"It took some convincing, but eventually the client stated that they were very happy not to have chosen any of the 'safer' proposals."

EIRIK SEU STOKKMO, SCANDINAVIAN DESIGN GROUP

Spam

DESIGN *Eirik Seu Stokkmo, Teipu*

To create a logo that would reflect the act of writing, without however lifting the pen from the page—that was the task that Norwegian designer Eirik Seu Stokkmo set himself for this personal project. Spam was an experimental project drawing on quotes from junk emails and using them for T-shirt and logo designs. Stokkmo thought Spam needed a logo that was similarly experimental, a quality that is shown typographically through the logo, without too much regard for how flexible, reproducible, or legible it is.

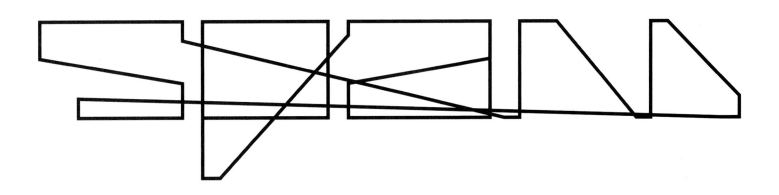

RULE 1... AND HOW TO BREAK IT!

The concept of the continuous line is as decipherable as the word that the line describes.

The Brand Union

ART DIRECTION *Wally Krantz,*
Executive Creative Director of
The Brand Union in New York
DESIGN *Jaime Burns*
ILLUSTRATION *Janice Kwa*
(icons and maps)

RULE 1... AND HOW TO BREAK IT!
If you want to convince clients
your work isn't going to be dull and
predictable, start with your own logo.

✟

F E E D B A C K
*"You aren't really following the
rules of corporate identity."*
A CLIENT

When a global brand consultancy decides to rebrand and design a logo, it knows that its work will be scrutinized closely. Enterprise IG, part of the WPP stable of companies, needed to reinvigorate itself and present a new image to the world, rebranding itself as The Brand Union. The identity itself was developed in the New York office by a team led by Wally Krantz, Executive Creative Director of The Brand Union for the USA. "The symbol was built from the counterforms of the letterforms that spell Brand Union," Krantz explains. "Like the people, offerings, and offices of The Brand Union, these shapes are working together and in the process of building." Rather than the bland, corporate, and safe logo some might have expected, this bold and different design was chosen, in which the counterforms of the letters are present in gray and cyan. Presented in negative space, the consultancy's name is not immediately legible, the choice having been made that a daring and distinct logo was more important. The forms of the logo were developed into an accompanying pattern and a world map, highlighting the consultancy's presence in offices around the world.

Thou shalt make the logo

app

Rule 2

Logos, it is held, should mirror and adopt the qualities of the organization or company they are for. But some of the design conventions used for certain business sectors can easily become stale and drift into cliché. By dashing expectations, the following logos make viewers engage with companies afresh.

ropriate

THE OFFICE OF
TONY BLAIR

DESIGN *Lucienne Roberts*

The Office of Tony Blair

RULE 2... AND HOW TO BREAK IT!
A conventional identity, while
appropriate to the role, would have
done a poor job of encapsulating the
character of a politician known as
much for his marketing and PR skills
as anything else.

The Office of Tony Blair

Tony Blair
PO Box 60519
London
W2 7JU
www.tonyblairoffice.org

PO Box 60519
London
W2 7JU
www.tonyblairoffice.org

The Office of Tony Blair

with compliments
www.tonyblairoffice.org

Following his successful rebranding of the British Labour Party and a decade-long term as a sometimes controversial Prime Minister, Tony Blair set up an office to deal with his various new interests—as well as public speaking engagements and consultancy work for banks and insurance companies, there are his foundations, teaching positions, and his role as Quartet Representative in the Middle East.

Lucienne Roberts, a well-respected and rather highbrow graphic designer, was asked to design an identity for what was now christened The Office of Tony Blair. It was to be used for stationery and online.

Think of statesmen and diplomats and the imagery that comes to mind generally involves ornate and fussy serif scripts and icons derived from heraldry or national flags. Asked however to come up with something modern yet uncontroversial, Roberts designed an identity that departs from these category norms.

A sans-serif font was deemed a step too far, and Roberts instead chose to steer a middle course by using Serifa, a slab serif designed in the 1960s. The choice of color palette also required steering a careful course to avoid the strong associations—political or otherwise—that many colors have. The final choice was ocher and gray, which, when overprinted, gives a third color. The milky white of the recycled paper used for the stationery is picked up as a buttermilk-colored masthead online.

Party

Notes on a Party
Events from the Inside Out

RULE 2... AND HOW TO BREAK IT!

By making the company name into a tagline accompanying the main logo, the designers have created an appropriate mood while also attracting attention in no uncertain terms.

Notes on a Party is a website based around event planning and entertaining. BaseNYC developed a logo that injects a bit of glamour into proceedings, as well as working across various platforms. To do so, they "zoomed in" on one word from the site's name—party—and made it quite literally the star of the show. This main image is supported by the site's full name, which becomes a sort of tagline (or a "signature or hostess," according to the designers). This in turn, depending on the application, is accompanied by another tagline—"Events from the Inside Out"—developed by Base's copywriting division, BaseWORDS. "As this venture is concerned primarily with event planning, we created a logo that plays on camera flashes, stars, and urban nightlife glitz," explain Base. In addition to appearing in animated form on the blog-like website—also designed by Base—the logo is used in static form on stationery, business cards, event invitations, and an e-newsletter.

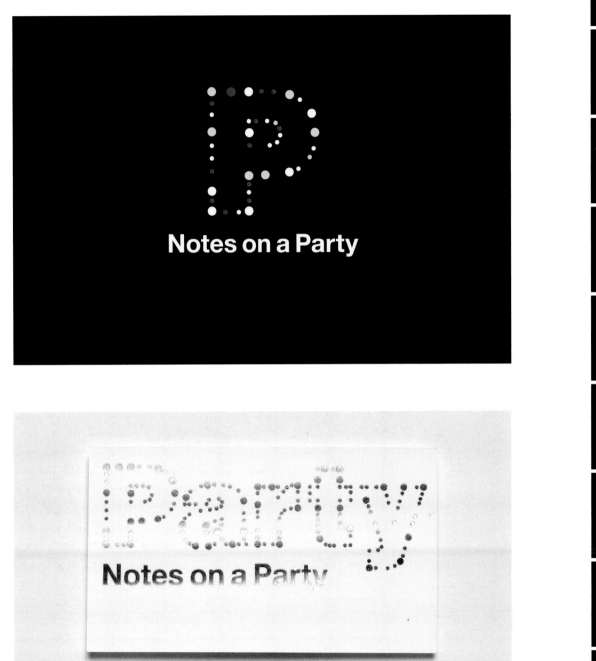

VERT FLUO

DESIGN *Julien Rivoire,*
Bastardgraphics

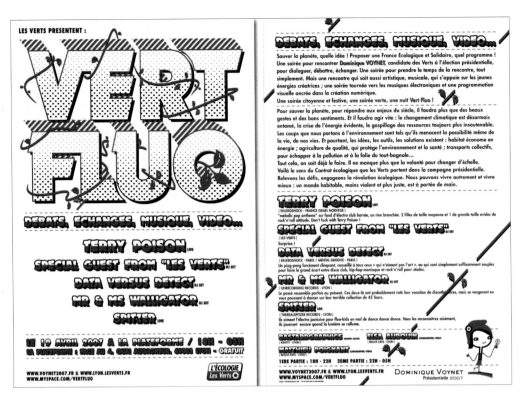

RULE 2... AND HOW TO BREAK IT!
As much a club night as a political meeting of the Green Party, this event needed imagery beyond the standard eco clichés in order to draw in the intended audience.

During the 2007 Presidential Election in France, a large event was held in the city of Lyon to present the Green Party's candidate, Dominique Voynet, with well-known DJs providing music alongside other artistic entertainments. The events organizers, Art Farty and Aimez-vous Brahms, asked local designer Julien Rivoire of Bastardgraphics to develop a logo for the event. Most "green" events rely on well-established "eco" iconography, but Rivoire wanted something that would incorporate an urban element alongside natural images such as foliage.

✠

FEEDBACK
"They liked it–I had no modifications to do.
They were like, 'perfect, this one is ace!'"

JULIEN RIVOIRE, BASTARDGRAPHICS

PRIMARY FLIGHT

DESIGN *BOOKSIIII, Blackbooks*

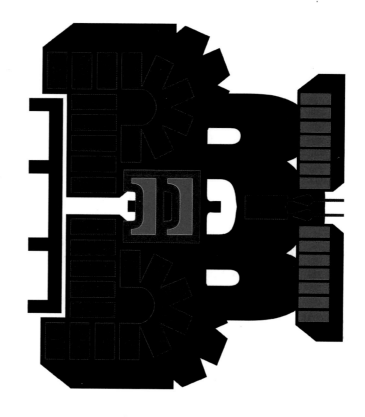

RULE 2... AND HOW TO BREAK IT!
When an idiom has become commercialized to the extent that graffiti and stenciling has, to use it for an exhibition that seeks to present "authentic" street art could be counterproductive.

In December 2007, the Wynwood Art District in Miami was home to a graffiti art festival that sought to restore the artform to its original outdoor location on concrete walls, as opposed to the walls of art galleries or retail spaces where it has become more usual. One of the curators was stencil artist BOOKSIIII, and his design group Blackbooks created a logo for the exhibition. The busy logo doesn't draw on graffiti art nor does it really draw on stenciling, and the name of the exhibition seems to have been the starting point for an abstract image that might have begun as an airplane. If anything it is early computer games that seem to be the reference.

BOXFRESH

ART DIRECTION *Ed Templeton*
DESIGN AND ILLUSTRATION
Annina Günter
Red Design

RULE 2... AND HOW TO BREAK IT!
By removing the straitjacket of
predictability, both logo and subject
can be seen in a new light. Who's
to say that an approach more usually
used for women's fashion can't work
for a housing estate?

Public housing in the UK is not always a thing of beauty. Deprivation and crime conspire with crumbling and neglected buildings to create some places that are unloved by their residents and known generally only as sites of social unrest. So the invitation to create logos reflecting "British Youth" that would work on T-shirts for fashion company Boxfresh was an opportunity for Red Design to question what is going on in these areas and play with preconceptions on all sides. "We decided to pick three of the UK's most notorious housing estates and turn them into something beautiful," says Annina Günter of Red Design. "By decorating the names of the housing estates, we remove them from their usual connotations and make people think." The swirly art nouveau style of the illustrations is a mile away from the 1960s, cheap modernist architecture found on these estates, but still employs the kind of austere, modernist typographical approach that people expect.

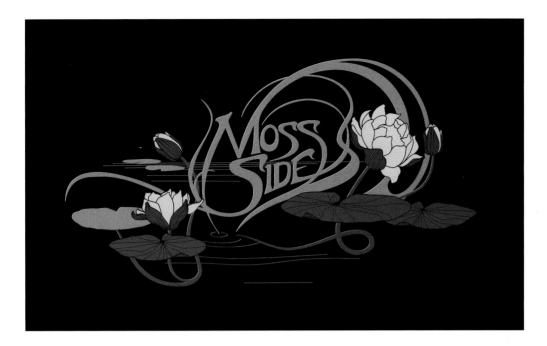

WE

ART DIRECTION *The Martin Agency*
DESIGN *Brian Collins, COLLINS*
TYPOGRAPHY *Chester Jenkins*

we can solve the climate crisis.

RULE 2... AND HOW TO BREAK IT!
Merging logo, strap line, and ad campaign into one creates a distinctive talking point and makes sure this logo always has its sleeves rolled up.

✝

FEEDBACK
The logo was honored with a dedicated feature in The New York Times.

Al Gore's Alliance for Climate Protection, the NGO founded with money from his Nobel Prize, needed a logo for a new campaign aiming to press home the urgency of addressing global warming. The Martin Agency was appointed to develop the campaign, and it in turn went to Brian Collins, who had just set up on his own after a long stint at Oglivy & Mather's Brand Innovation Group in New York. Rather than refer to the Alliance, the campaign was given its own name—We—and the logo underlined the campaign's message by substituting an inverted "m" for the "w," so that the concepts of "me" and "we" are intertwined. A soft and friendly typeface was commissioned from typographer Chester Jenkins. A supporting website and ad campaign was developed under the rubric "We can solve it."

CROSSINGS ARCHITECTURE

DESIGN *Francheska Guerrero,*
Unfolding Terrain

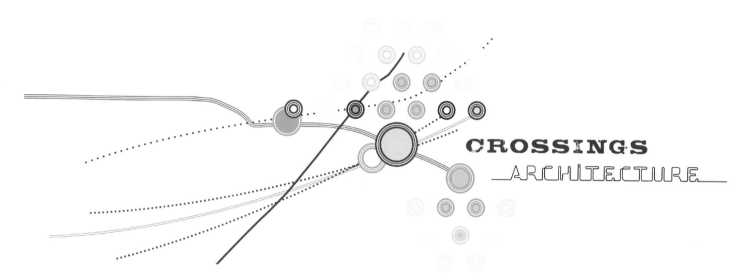

RULE 2... AND HOW TO BREAK IT!
Confounding expectations
can sometimes grab attention
very successfully—a bit like the
politician's trick of speaking
quietly in a noisy room.

Think about identities for architects and immediately you presume right angles, clean shapes, and bold modernist outlines. But when Francheska Guerrero of Unfolding Terrain was asked by Michigan-based Crossings Architecture to develop an identity for them, the practice stipulated "no classic Futura." Instead they asked for something that was "progressive, both in form and typography."

So Guerrero went for two unusual typefaces to give an idiosyncratic combination of low-fi and hi-tech: Chase, a low-fi slab serif suggestive of the typeface used on metal letterpresses, and Echelon, a typeface which references handwriting and continuous bent metal letters. The resulting logo ended up being pretty abstract. Employing very fine, delicate line art, it's a logo that is visually light and organic rather than geometric in feel. "The goal was to move beyond the conventions of current and historical logo design, both in form and typography," says Guerrero.

FREE

ART DIRECTION *Dan McQue and Luther Spicer*
DESIGNER *Kellé Hinton*
IE Design Consultancy

RULE 2... AND HOW TO BREAK IT!

If you have a difficult task, there's nothing like an ambush to make people wake up and take notice.

✠

FEEDBACK
"Love the idea of 'bombing' that comes through and the immediacy of the graffiti style."
UCCF

Christian Unions promote Christianity in the universities and colleges of the UK, and their umbrella body is called UCCF: The Christian Unions. One of its initiatives was to design a new version of Mark's Gospel and target 400,000 students with no previous exposure to the Bible. It was to be heavily and distinctly branded in a way that would break through young people's expectations of religious texts. The logo would not only be printed on the front of this edition of Mark's Gospel, but would also be used for the initiative as a whole.

IE Design Consultancy took what they describe as the most "downmarket and ubiquitous of materials—graffiti and Helvetica" to come up with the finished logo. "We were fascinated by the practice of 'bombing' where artists spray over each other's work as part of an ongoing visual conversation. Using spray cans and stencils we set the word 'free' in our client's corporate font—Helvetica." A logo kit is on UCCF's website along with brand guidelines, allowing young missionaries access to easy downloads to create their own posters and communications.

Svet in Dom, SNG Maribor

DESIGN *Uros Lehner, Ookie*

RULE 2... AND HOW TO BREAK IT!
Using an idiom from popular culture makes this highbrow event seem lively and accessible.

✝

FEEDBACK
The logo impressed the judges enough to win an open call for entries.

The Slovene National Theatre has its home in an imposing neoclassical building in the historic center of Maribor, Slovenia's second city, which lies close to the Austrian border. In 2006, it programmed a season of plays with the title of Svet in Dom, which translates as "world and home," reflecting the fact that there were to be three plays by foreign playwrights and three by local ones. The theater put out a call for entries for logos for the season, and local designer Uros Lehner's proposal—a distinctly handmade logo—won.

Lehner says he deliberately set out to make "something different." Rather than using existing typefaces, letters were cut out of colored paper or drawn crudely using felt-tip pens, and the results were then scanned and vectorized. The words look almost as though they have been knitted. Six different color applications were developed for each of the six plays, and the hues and the homespun typography are suggestive of 1950s cartoons.

THE OPTIMIST (WWW. OPTIMISTWORLD.COM)

ART DIRECTION, DESIGN, AND ILLUSTRATION *Emma Morton,* *LOVE*

RULE 2... AND HOW TO BREAK IT!

If a brand wants to say something different, then it needs to look different. Looking more like something culled from a children's book, the bird character works more effectively than any traditional newspaper logo would in this context.

The Optimist is an online news website "dedicated to taking a daily look on the bright side." While most news websites tend to have solemn identities and logos based on the mastheads of famous, long-established newspapers, The Optimist has an illustrated, hand-drawn logo of a little yellow bird. Called The Optimist, this little creature flits around "spreading good news everywhere he goes." The Optimist is principally a platform to showcase the work of some of the smaller, less well-funded charities, and is itself operated as a charity, hence the emphasis on positive developments rather than hard news.

"I wanted the execution to be lighthearted and friendly. The phrase 'a little birdie told me' led me to create a chirpy character that spreads good news," says Emma Morton at LOVE. "The logo is a world away from the other news and charity logos in that it is hand-drawn, friendly, and fun. The logo also adapts for different subcategories. For example, the sports bird is holding a tennis racket. But they still feel like a set."

"The client loved the character and felt it portrayed everything they wanted to say. They also felt that it was flexible enough to develop with them as a company."

EMMA MORTON, LOVE

Kutina

DESIGN *Boris Ljubicic,*
Studio International

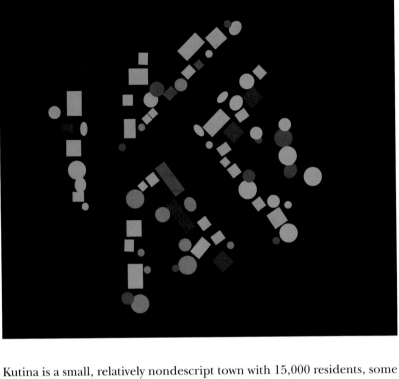

RULE 2... AND HOW TO BREAK IT!
A heraldic image is what you might
have expected, but for a town with
an image problem, that would have
done little to make it stand out or
state its ambitions.

Kutina is a small, relatively nondescript town with 15,000 residents, some 30 miles (50km) east of the Croatian capital Zagreb, and perhaps best known for its petrochemical works. So coming up with an identity for the place wasn't an easy task for Boris Ljubicic of Zagreb-based Studio International. As Ljubicic felt there was little by way of preexisting imagery or identity to build on, he had to start from scratch. The logo he produced is both abstract and literal—the letter "K" (in medium weight Helvetica) is reimagined as a mapping out of streets, as if in an architect's model of urban planning. The whited-out "K" then has a series of buildings and trees running alongside it, defining the space. It is a simple logo that exists in different colorways, and which always has the option to become three-dimensional, either for real or simulated by adding shadows to the fictional structures. The overall feel of the logo is more suggestive of a creative company, such as a publisher or architect's studio, than a sleepy, industrial provincial town.

ABIERTO

DESIGN *Diego Hurtado de Mendoza*

Abierto is Spanish for "open," and that was the name given to a series of exhibitions organized by the Colegio Oficial de Arquitectos de Madrid in which six different architectural studios showed their most recent projects. "The graphic image was all black and white and the main logo just tried to highlight the idea of 'openness,'" says designer Diego Hurtado de Mendoza. While the main logo doesn't use the full name of the exhibition, relying instead simply on its first letter modified with a keyhole, the designer had a second bite of the cherry when it came to the accompanying DVDs. The DVD packaging includes a different logo with a literal "open" sign printed on the disc.

RULE 2... AND HOW TO BREAK IT!
If your design is clean and strong enough, perhaps the name can be implied rather than spelled out?

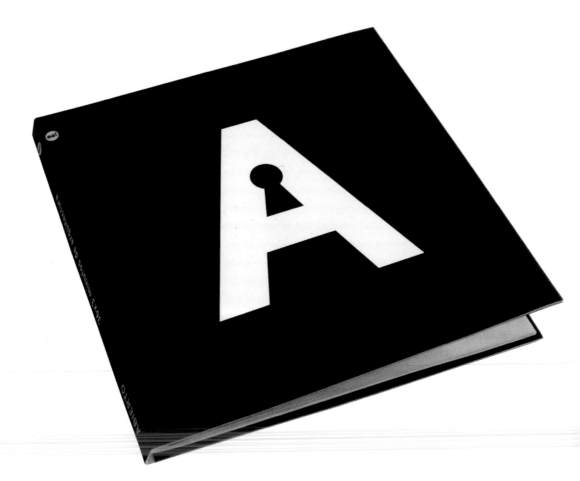

A

✣

FEEDBACK

"The simplicity of the graphic solution made the newborn series of exhibitions very visible and they quickly became a regular meeting point for the architects of Madrid."

DIEGO HURTADO DE MENDOZA

ABIERTO
36x3 minutos de arquitectura

DVD editado a partir de los videos elaborados por 36 equipos de arquitectos de Madrid en los que reflexionan sobre su obra dentro del ciclo de exposiciones ABIERTO en la Fundación COAM, 2005-2006.

ea! ediciones de arquitectura

8 436039 069626

D. L: BI-2015-07

ABIERTO

LIGHTSTREAM ANIMATION

ART DIRECTION *John Helms*
DESIGN *Von Glitschka,*
Glitschka Studios

RULE 2... AND HOW TO BREAK IT!
Rather than work backward from CGI, a traditional logo forms a strong and effective platform for animation as well as company recognition.

Lightstream Pictures is an established movie company that set up a new animation and effects studio in Petaluma, California. The call went to self-styled "illustrative designer" Von Glitschka, who accepted the brief with a tight deadline of just five days. While the cute, smile-inducing result may not be unusual for branding other kinds of companies, Glitschka suggests the approach—starting with a logo in the conventional sense—was a departure for a special effects company.

"I played off the name of the company and used a character-based metaphor, a firefly," explains Glitschka. "This character has obvious attributes that lend themselves to the client's name and genre of work they do. Most effects companies bypass traditional logo design and go straight to CGI. I wanted to avoid that. The logo had to work well in 2-D before it was fleshed out in 3-D. I also wanted a mark that would build a brand via its animation potential as well."

McGregor's Solicitors

DESIGN *Dave Sedgwick, 999 Design*

RULE 2... AND HOW TO BREAK IT!
If your client doesn't want to be just another face in the crowd, let the logo signal their intentions.

Think of law firms, and you generally think of logos that are as stuffy and pompous as the lawyers that run them. But McGregor's Solicitors is one law firm that had the confidence to go in a very unusual direction. Rather than a verbose "corporate" identity, Dave Sedgwick devised a simple mark that stands on its own. It's vaguely reminiscent of a snatch of cursive script or a legal ribbon, and certainly unlike any other lawyer's logo.

THE SONIC CARD

DESIGN *Dave Sedgwick, 999 Design*

RULE 2... AND HOW TO BREAK IT!

Check with the client; they may want to target new customers, so give them something outside their usual aesthetic.

The BBC Philharmonic Orchestra regularly stage events across the UK, running workshops for young musicians and performing their wide-ranging repertoire. To that end, they set up a membership club to promote events and use the opportunity to widen their target market by appealing to a young audience. While classical music is generally presumed to be stuffy or old fashioned, in this instance the color scheme and illustration are totally contemporary. Art director Dave Sedgwick explains, "I feel what's different about this is that it doesn't instantly say 'classical music' and could just as easily be for a club night, new bar, or fashion label."

Conservative Party

DESIGN *Perfect Day*

RULE 2... AND HOW TO BREAK IT!
Logos sometimes have to work hard. To shift stubborn perceptions about the nature of this political party, the logo had to mark a radical departure that would get potential voters questioning the thinking behind it.

✝

F E E D B A C K
"I have seen better from a four-year-old with a box of crayons."

"This is brave, not careless. It is something I can get behind."

"This is just a wishy-washy symbol designed to offend as few people as possible, while inspiring none."

CONTRASTING VIEWS FROM DIFFERENT CONSERVATIVE PARTY FORUMS

The British Conservative Party wanted to emulate the rebrand that had seen its rival, the Labour Party, trounce it in successive general elections. The Conservatives had continued to use a torch logo, originally designed in the Margaret Thatcher era by Michael Peters, but its aggressive, fascistic overtones were out of sync with the softer public face being promoted by new party leader David Cameron. So a new logo was commissioned from a low-profile graphic design consultancy, Perfect Day, which ignored the fact that British politics had always been rigidly color coded, with Labour aligned with red and the Conservatives with blue. As in many other countries, the color green was inextricably associated with the Green Party and other ecological groups. The logo devised for the Conservatives now featured a green oak tree, intended to signify "strength, endurance, and renewal." And while its innocuous informal and sketchy style may have been entirely unremarkable if used for a provincial beauty salon, it was a bit of a departure for a major political party.

LV=

ART DIRECTION *Nina Jenkins*
DESIGN *Michael Paisley*
and Robert Young
The Partners

RULE 2... AND HOW TO BREAK IT!
If you want to convince people
you are different, don't look like
your competitors.

✝

FEEDBACK
"The fresh, vibrant brand enhances
our ambitious plans for growth and
supports our aim of improving the
long-term value of the society to
its members."

DAVID RANFORD, GROUP MARKETING DIRECTOR, LV=

Liverpool Victoria is an insurance and savings company that had been laboring under its slightly frumpy, nineteenth-century name. It approached The Partners, looking to rejuvenate itself with a new brand identity, personality, and tone of voice. The Partners decided to retain the company's heritage, but abbreviate the name and make it more memorable. And as the new brand personality was to be "sharp with a heart," the "V" was rendered as a heart. The organization's mutual structure was incorporated into the logo by use of the equals sign, which also allowed a natural segue to its many businesses and partners. Financial services branding normally plays things very safe, but by using symbols to create an iconic logo rather than a name, LV= did indeed seek a very different solution. A deferential nod in the direction of Milton Glaser's famous I Love New York logo is undeniable, and while a similar approach has been picked up in a variety of sectors, it is very unusual for financial services.

BOY BASTIAENS

DESIGN *Boy Bastiaens*

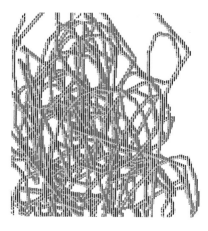

RULE 2... AND HOW TO BREAK IT!
Graphic designers are as likely to fall prey to predictability when they design for themselves as when they do so for corporate clients, but it doesn't always need to be the case.

As is so often the case, it is when designers create their own logos that they can be most experimental. Dutch graphic designer Boy Bastiaens took the bold step of having a messy scribble represent him to the world. "Though it is a visual cliché in its own way, I think it won't be very appealing or attractive to a lot of designers to have their trade associated with 'messy' doodling," says Bastiaens. But behind the doodle there is a coherent idea that speaks about the design process itself. According to Bastiaens, it's "an abstract image of entangled threads, a knot, that needs to be unraveled to get a clear line." Once he had settled on the idea, actually drawing the right image was the hard part. What looks like a kid's crayon dragged over a textured surface or a ball of wool is actually a complicated image made up of vertical lines. However, interrogating the image too much doesn't help, as it is so abstract.

Rule 3

IDENTITIES ARE USUALLY EXPECTED TO BE FIXED, SOLID, AND IMMUTABLE. BRANDS OFTEN PUT CONSIDERABLE EFFORT INTO ENSURING THEIR IDENTITY REMAINS THE SAME AND IS NOT DILUTED OR MODIFIED IN ANY WAY. BUT A MORE OPEN AND CASUAL APPROACH CAN BE JUST AS EFFECTIVE.

Thou shalt make a marque That Is constant and unchanging.

Casa da Música

ART DIRECTION *Stefan Sagmeister*
DESIGN *Matthias Ernstberger and Quentin Walesch*
LOGO GENERATOR *Ralph Ammer*

RULE 3… AND HOW TO BREAK IT!
Allowing flexibility permits all facets of an organization to be expressed. And if one element of a logo is strong enough, the rest of it can be thrown open.

The Casa da Música, a concert hall in the city of Porto in northern Portugal, is a stunning example of the prowess of superstar architect Rem Koolhaas. It is a building with an intriguing geometry, defining a space formed by strong, unpredictable lines. Stefan Sagmeister, as renowned in the world of graphics as Koolhaas is in architecture, was asked to come up with an identity for this iconic building. His solution is as thought provoking and controversial as the building itself, but it was a process he found far from simple. "Our initial desire to design an identity without featuring the building proved impossible because, as we studied the structure, we realized that the building itself is a logo," he says. Koolhaas calls this "the organization of issues of symbolism."

Sagmeister decided to adopt a different tack, developing a flexible form derived from the building's shape. A "logo generator" system was used, which allows the colors to be selected by the user for whatever application is required. The concert hall is home to performances of many kinds, from early music and symphonic music to jazz and world music; Sagmeister and his team wanted a logo that could change its character in the same way that the hall itself changes according to the kind of music being performed. "We tried to avoid another rendering of a building by developing a system where this recognizable, unique, modern form transforms itself like a chameleon from application to application, changes from media to media where the physical building itself is the ultimate (very high-res) rendering in a long line of logos," is how Sagmeister describes this fluid identity.

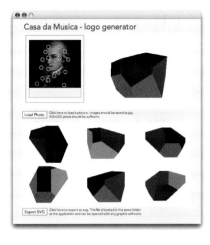

Casa da Musica - logo generator

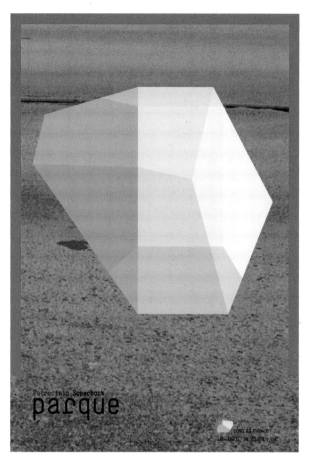

Patrocínio Superback
parque

SERVIÇO
EDUCATIVO
'07

casa da música

2º ANIVERSÁRIO
CASA DA MÚSICA

casa da música

✝

F E E D B A C K

"The logotype is just plain terrible."

ANONYMOUS RESPONSE ON A BLOG

Ann-Sofie Axelsson

DESIGN *Hjärta Smärta*

RULE 3... AND HOW TO BREAK IT!
There is no reason why a logo should always be thought of in terms of paper and two dimensions. Why not just give the client a good reason to wear it?

FEEDBACK
"Ann-Sofie loves her logotype! The logotype is wearable and follows her wherever she goes."

HJÄRTA SMÄRTA

In a world that is increasingly obsessed with celebrities and reality TV, personal branding seems as essential as it is controversial. But this was something altogether less problematic for artist and exhibition producer Ann-Sofie Axelsson. What she wanted was simply a graphic profile made up of a logotype, stationery, and a home page for her website. To this, her friends, the Swedish design duo Hjärta Smärta, tasked with the design and knowing her intimately, added shoes. Not just any shoes, but shoes that encapsulated the branding and were an essential part of the graphic identity. The exclamation point after the "A" of the primary logotype lends itself to reinterpretation as an actual set of high heel shoes. This then became a very portable and distinctive bit of branding, and is more memorable than a business card. Likewise the red exclamation point can pop up anywhere and immediately imply Axelsson's presence.

Matteria

DESIGN *Emmi Salonen, EMMI*

matteria

RULE 3... AND HOW TO BREAK IT!

There is a fine line between a logo that morphs and a brand system, but who cares as long as it works?

✢

FEEDBACK

"The method proved systematic, analytical, and possessed a fresh character"

ANU SUOMINEN AND MONICA POTVIN, MATTERIA

Matteria is a company with bases in Spain and Finland, selling a variety of home accessories that have been selected to meet a set of stringent ecological criteria, as well as being aesthetically pleasing. London-based designer Emmi Salonen was asked to come up with an identity, a website, and various other materials for Matteria that would project the company's environmental friendliness. "It was clear from the start that the logo and identity design would need to adhere to the same environmental principles. The brand pattern reflects the cycles in nature with the use of recycled and environmentally friendly material throughout all the applications," explains Salonen. "There is not one logo mark, but a continuous change of patterns and marks based on four basic shapes, just like the continuous cycles in nature, where nothing is ever the same."

Diil

DESIGN *Paul Barlow, L&CO Design*

AAABBCCCDDDEEEFFF
GGGHHHIIIJJJKKKLLL
MMMNNNOOOPPPQQQ
RRRSSSTTTUUUVVV
WWWXXXYYYZZZ

111222333444555
666777888999000

@@>˂£3()[]%%&$!?=
.,'';;❉❊◔◔◔'.'——+

ÅÂÄÀÁÃ ÊËÈÉÊ ÏÎÍÏ
ÔÖÕÔÓ ÜÙÛÚÜ ÑÝ

TM ™ ™ ™
©©®®©®

"Diil" means deal in Estonian, and was chosen as the name of a new cellphone operator to run alongside the premium service of its parent company, EMT (Estonian Mobile Telecommunications). As Diil is a value brand, Paul Barlow of London-based L&CO Design decided to go for a "cheap and cheerful" positioning with a hand-drawn logo. "We wanted to create a brand that had stacks of personality but was almost antibrand, brought to you by some guy from a garage in Tallinn," says Barlow. While the hand-drawn typography and green background remain constant, the peripheral design elements are varied and can be chosen more or less at will, depending on the situation and the whim of the user. A series of small hand-drawn icons are provided to be added as part of the Diil branding, which is flexible enough to accommodate further hand-drawn doodles by whoever is implementing it at the time.

The letters making up the logo were taken from alphabets hand-drawn in both Roman and Cyrillic (for Estonia's large-Russian speaking community). The result was cheekily named Diil Bold Collapsed, as if it were a formal typeface, when in fact it is a shakily executed tracing from Helvetica Bold. The irreverent approach was aimed at the younger end of the market, and the logo's flexibility sends a strong message about the company's tariff structure.

RULE 3… AND HOW TO BREAK IT!

If you have an identity that is
strong enough, you can accommodate
flexibility. Here it allows an engaging
informality that is perfect for its
target market.

FEEDBACK

*Diil has taken a good market share
and has become something of a cult
brand in Estonia.*

KOAN

ART DIRECTION AND DESIGN
Adam Rix, LOVE
ILLUSTRATION *Stuart Simmons*

RULE 3... AND HOW TO BREAK IT!
Allowing an identity to vary for each employee, and even letting them design it, sends a message more powerfully than a single logo could.

✝

FEEDBACK
"The client was so happy with the idea that it staged a two-day workshop out of the office for all the staff to create the logos. The logos now also hang on the office walls as canvas artwork."

ADAM RIX, LOVE

It is not uncommon for companies to say the creativity of their staff is at the center of what they do. While this usually remains a platitude, when it came to Koan, an ethical public relations company based in the north of England, they decided to put their identity where their mouth was. Briefed to design a logo that would reflect the creativity of Koan's staff, Adam Rix at LOVE proposed an open-ended identity system where each member of the company's staff would draw their own versions of the logo. The client lapped up the idea of every employee literally creating and expressing his or her own identity. Everyone was given a template of the word "Koan" hand-drawn over the top of Futura, and then asked to embellish it. Illustrator Stuart Simmons was then given the results and redrew them so that there would be a consistent feel across the many embellishments. Each member of staff had their own design put on their business card, while the rest of the logos went into a "brand tool kit."

"I love identity systems where there is no fixed logo, where the logo shifts and changes for each execution," says Rix. "If what Koan said was true about its people, then it was the only real way to communicate their individuality and creativity."

KREA Expresión Contemporanea

DESIGN *Pablo Rubio, Erretres Diseño*

RULE 3... AND HOW TO BREAK IT!
Allowing the identity to take a variety of forms engages the viewer and exemplifies the creativity of an artistic entity such as the KREA center.

✠

F E E D B A C K
The client threw a big party for the launch of the logo, and it was given widespread coverage in the local media.

KREA Expresión Contemporanea (or KREA Contemporary Expression) is the name of an ambitious new cultural center in Vitoria-Gasteiz, capital of the province of Alava in the semiautonomous Basque region in northern Spain. The project is bankrolled by the charitable foundation of local financial institution Caja Vital Kutxa, and has its home in a former seventeenth-century convent to which a modern snaking glass structure is being added. The hope is that the center will become a major cultural attraction and have a similar regenerative effect to that of the now famous Guggenheim Museum in nearby Bilbao, as well as providing an impetus to local artists and musicians.

Madrid-based consultancy Erretres Diseño developed a logo that would be effective in a variety of applications, from the signage to the website of the institute. Their idea was for a logo that was inherently unstable. Rather than letters or typeforms sitting on a grid, as is more usually the case, in this design the letters making up the logo are formed out of grids, and these grids mutate, as does the logo itself. It is as if the letters, rather than being printed, are made of the electronic displays used at airports or train stations. Likewise, the color is not stable, and while light blue is the foundation color, the logo can draw upon a palette of four colors, or can be split into two for the exterior signage. As such the logo reflects the multifarious activities of the center itself as it mutates. The inherent flexibility in the brand meant that Erretres was able to design button badges for the launch party, featuring just the grids, but not the name.

KREA is a play on the Spanish word for creation (crea), but spelled with a K to give it an inflection of Basque, the language of many of the people in the area.

SEED MEDIA GROUP

ART DIRECTION *Stefan Sagmeister*
DESIGNER *Matthias Ernstberger*
Sagmeister Inc.

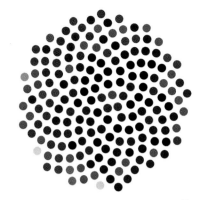

seed media group**.**

RULE 3... AND HOW TO BREAK IT!
The changes the logo goes through
reflect important aspects of the
company, meaning it reinforces
rather than dilutes the brand.

✠

FEEDBACK
The company has a showcase on its
website proudly explaining the logo,
where it can also be downloaded.

A publisher of scientific magazines, books, and films, Seed Media Group wanted an identity that reflected its business of engaging with science through culture. Stefan Sagmeister and his team decided on an approach that would embody this. "We were looking for something open-ended and flexible, a vessel we could fill with new meanings as they developed," says the studio. "The identity is based on phyllotaxis, a form found everywhere from seashells to Greek architecture, from pineapples to the Sydney opera house, gazelles' horns to the optimum curve a highway turns. It plays a role in biology, zoology, botany, medicine, physics, geometry, and math. It's in the golden ratio and golden curve."

Like Stefan Sagmeister's identity for the Casa da Musica (see pages 74–75), this is a chameleon identity, taking on the colors of what is around it. So on business cards, the small "seeds" that make up the identity turn out on closer inspection to be an image of the person whose card it is. On letterheads, iridescent inks used to print the logo reflect the immediate vicinity, and on the company's website it takes a low-key presence as if it were a stamp, or a dandelion head gone to seed.

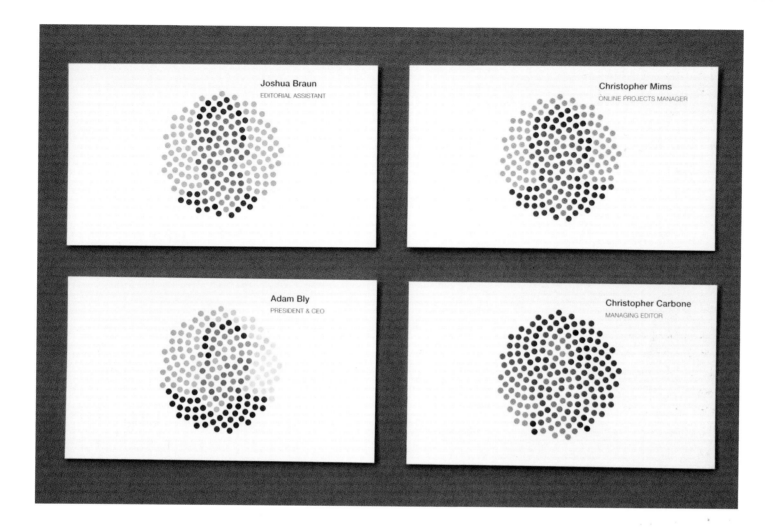

DARLINGS OF THE DAY

ART DIRECTION *Blair Thomson*
DESIGN *Paul Warren*
biz-R

RULE 3... AND HOW TO BREAK IT!
Remaining true to the spirit of
the band in this case meant throwing
constancy to the wind, something
that only works because of the
distinctiveness of the various
elements that make up the identity.

Darlings Of The Day are an emerging alternative rock band based in Los Angeles. They wanted an identity that reflected their style and sound, and that could also be easily reproduced on various pieces of merchandise and apparel. Above all, it had to be something that was a little bit different and unconventional. UK-based design consultancy biz-R came up with a solution that wasn't so much a logo as an assemblage of readily identifiable elements that could be configured in different ways to present an identity in continuous evolution. The different logo forms could be used for different seasons and could be used to represent different band themes or tour dates. It is an approach that lends itself as readily to a T-shirt graphic as to an animation on the web.

DESIGN IS PLAY

DESIGN *Angie Wang and Mark Fox, Design is Play*

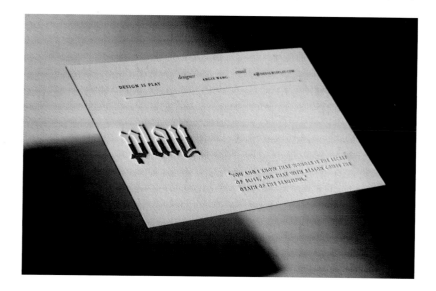

RULE 3... AND HOW TO BREAK IT!
The act of printing and remaking will always result in differences, however small, and that's something that this logo or series of logos picks up and runs with.

When San Francisco–based graphic design studio Design is Play got round to designing their own logo, Angie Wang and Mark Fox decided to push the boat out a bit. What they ended up with was a series of cryptic marks that pointed in their company's direction rather than a unitary logo. The various fragments, relying on the technique of debossing and drawing on an ornate Gothic script, were however clearly suggestive of the world of graphic design and printing. And by adopting a name such as Design is Play for their studio, Wang and Fox were slightly honor bound to come up with something innovative.

"'Play' can be understood as freedom of movement within a defined space," they explain. "The identity plays with ink and its absence: black fills only a portion of the debossed logotype, and the inked areas vary from piece to piece. The logotype is based on a late fifteenth-century English Gothic Blackletter redrawn from a brass original by Frank Chouteau Brown and published in 1902."

As a result, "there is no 'one' official version of the wordmark," they add. "Also, the wordmark is designed to be seen in an inked and debossed form, not in an ink-only form which is typical of most logos." It's an approach which lends their stationery a slightly sculptural quality.

Institut Parfumeur Flores

DESIGN *Bunch Design*

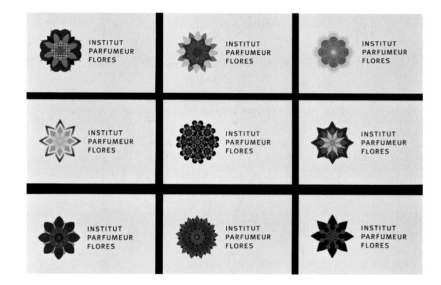

RULE 3... AND HOW TO BREAK IT!

There is constancy of a sort here—every presentation of the company's name is accompanied by a flower. It just so happens that it's not necessarily the same flower each time, piquing interest and delight in the viewer.

Designing a corporate identity and logo for a perfumery is a bit of a gift of a job. While some of the most famous typographic logos come from the historic giants of this sector (think Yves Saint Laurent), Bunch Design's approach for this Croatian perfumery is more illustrative and free. Alongside a plain and unassuming sans serif presentation of the company's name, a wide variety of flower designs function as interchangeable icons that can be used either in conjunction with each other or as single alternatives, in a way that suggests infinite variety. It's an approach that lends itself nicely to stationery design, and the diversity of the imagery suggests the richness of nature itself, while essentially just daring to be sweet and pretty.

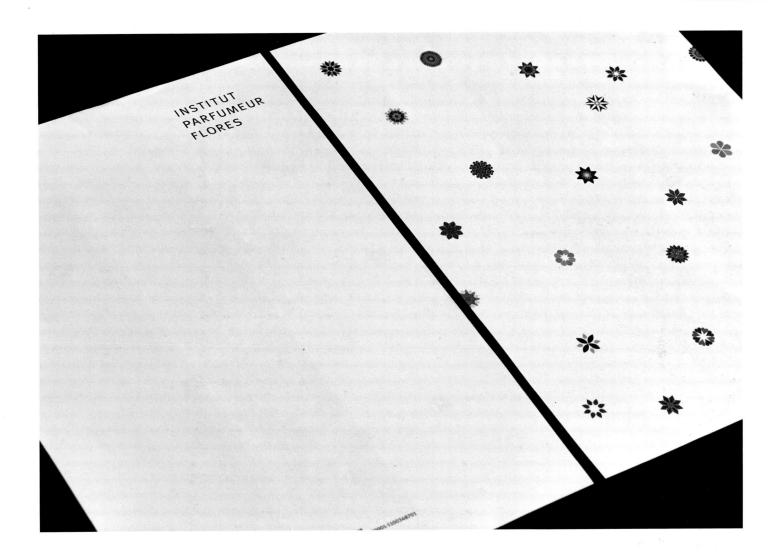

INSTITUT
PARFUMEUR
FLORES

KØBENHAVNS NATURSKOLER

DESIGN *Peter Graabaek, Kursiv*

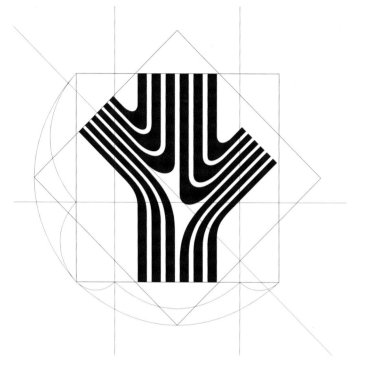

RULE 3... AND HOW TO BREAK IT!

When the theme is all about growth and development, why shouldn't the logo grow and grow as well?

✝

FEEDBACK

"The children loved playing with the stickers that made up the logo."

PETER GRAABAEK, KURSIV

What could be more appropriate from the homeland of Lego than a logo that is modular and takes its form from kids taking different bits and sticking them together? Københavns Naturskoler (Copenhagen Natureschools) is a large-scale initiative from the city council of the Danish capital Copenhagen, that takes teaching out of the classroom and into the countryside outside the city. In response to the invitation to develop a visual identity for the project, Peter Graabaek at graphic design practice Kursiv decided to junk the usual idea of a static logo. Instead he proposed a solution of "growing your own logo," a logo that would "sprout." It is a mark that is designed to fit with different sizes of itself, mimicking the structures and geometry of the natural world. It does so in a way that would entice the interest of the children themselves, for whom it could act as a puzzle-like game. It is also an approach that didn't interfere with the simple heraldic image for Copenhagen city council, which also features on some of the communications.

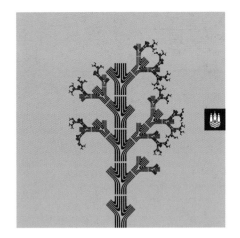

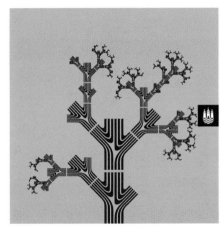

Photo by Torben Nielsen

LIVING BRASIL

DESIGN *Cako Martin*

RULE 3... AND HOW TO BREAK IT!
Web-based identities have no reason
to keep still, and here the changes
are tightly integrated with the theme
at hand.

Living Brasil is an internet portal promoting design, in particular interior design, to a wide spectrum of Brazilians (not only the rich who can usually afford to think of such things). The logo has to function as a masthead for the site, and Cako Martin, a Spaniard resident in São Paulo, wanted the design to be attractive enough so as not be eclipsed by the other items on the website (www.livingbrasil.com.br). While architecture and culture are also featured on the site, it is interior design that is its primary focus. So the logo that Martin designed gets a fresh interior design each time a new page opens. It appears in six different color permutations. The first time you see the logo on the site's home page, it is animated, appearing to be a room that is first painted and then furnished with a chair.

M31

DESIGN *Ian Lynam*

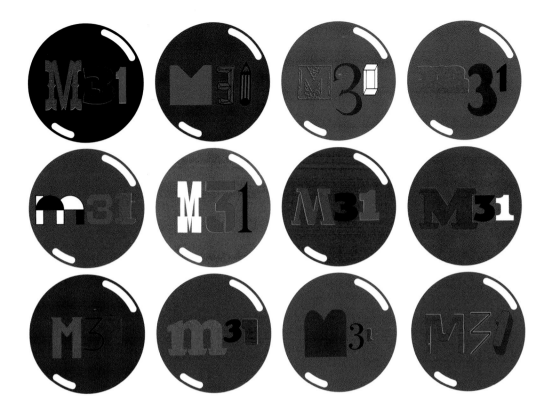

RULE 3… AND HOW TO BREAK IT!

If the client has capability and confidence in design, why not allow them to take part in the creation of the identity on an ongoing basis?

✝

F E E D B A C K

"The client loved it and has fully implemented the identity."

IAN LYNAM

M31 is a creative and production agency based in Tokyo, which approached Ian Lynam, a local graphic designer originally from the US, to come up with an identity. Given the agency's design literacy, Lynam proposed a flexible if predetermined package rather than a single logo, or what he calls a "modular logo super-family." "The client was given a kit of parts that they can use to remix their logo in innumerable variations," he explains. Other than a circle containing the letter M and numerals 31, the identity was thrown open like a box of candy.

"I wanted to explore the idea that a logo can be something as far away as possible from the typical modernist solution, as well as creating a logo that the design-conscious client can actively engage with," says Lynam. "It breaks with traditional ideas of a single 'answer' to a design 'problem.'"

Made in Bunch

DESIGN *Various designers*

RULE 3… AND HOW TO BREAK IT!

If a logo is meant to direct attention, in this case to graphic design, then what could be more effective than this master class of what design can do? After all, not every entity needs branding in the conventional static sense, especially not a design collective.

Creating their own logos is often the time when designers feel maximum license to experiment and push the boundaries. But Bunch Design, a graphic design collective with bases in London, Zagreb, and Singapore, decided to go one better and harness the talents of the designers they admire. It was, in short, to be a collaborative redesign.

"We decided that it was time to rework our corporate identity and base it around the overarching theme of 'Made in Bunch,'" the dedicated website explained, before the following entreaty: "Much of our work is predicated by the influences we as a collective of designers take from the world around us. So we thought we'd ask other designers how they see us and reflect this in our identity." The basic logo was put up for download and designers were asked to come up with whatever they wanted. "You might rubber stamp it, create an overdrawing, or simply cut it up and burn it, but we'd like you to sign it when you're done smashing it up," the collective asked.

The idea captured the imagination of designers and the response was enthusiastic. Hundreds of suggestions rolled in, with creations from design heroes such as Stefan Sagmeister, Malcom Garrett, Jonathan Ellery, and Carlos Segura mixing it with lesser knowns in an exciting and diverse master class of the kind of logo designs that graphic designers can come up with when set free from the usual constraints. We here feature some of the more rule-breaking logos, but it would be fair to say many of the designers took the opportunity to play free and easy.

The project is ongoing (its dedicated website is www.madeinbunch.com) and has spawned several pieces of merchandise, including a tote bag, T-shirt, and coffee mugs. And for a design collective, what could be more appropriate than having a sprawling, nonstop identity that features the talents of many different designers?

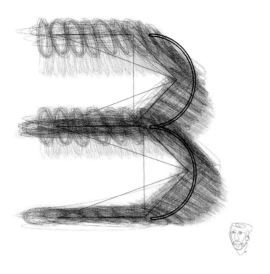

THOU SHALT MAKE A MARQUE THAT IS CONSTANT AND UNCHANGING

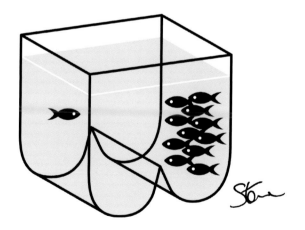

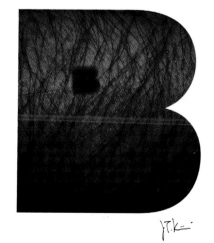

Sister Safia

DESIGN *Amy Stafford, Studio Blixa 6*

RULE 3... AND HOW TO BREAK IT!
If the ingredients are strong enough, a logo or a chutney will remain readily identifiable in many different forms.

✝

FEEDBACK
Safia had good responses from clients and contacts, with the British in particular getting the joke.

Based in Berlin, Sister Safia is a PR consultant working in the field of the contemporary arts market. As a freelance PR, her first task was to show that she is able to market herself effectively. So she turned to Amy Stafford at Studio Blixa 6 to help her with a self-promotional campaign that she wanted to develop into a visual identity for herself. She also wanted a design that could be used for various applications, from packaging, post, or business cards to a website. Safia's campaign, says Stafford, was based around the idea of "homemade chutneys, using them to build awareness of her own cheeky loudmouth" and spreading some "sunshine on the sourpuss Germans who need a little spice in their life."

As the daughter of a Tanzanian diplomat, Safia has spent time in India, England, and various African countries. Stafford decided to draw on this multicultural background to come up with a visual identity that operates as an assemblage of motifs rather than a fixed logo. "I applied graphic elements borrowed from Safia's cultural heritage and applied a pink, brown, and orange color scheme to reflect her time in India," says Stafford, adding that the dense text expresses "Safia's unique ability to fill every millimeter of space with words."

CAPITAL VIEW

DESIGN *Stereo*

RULE 3... AND HOW TO BREAK IT!

This is a company that is all about many different viewpoints, so having an identity that can morph and change allows it to express itself effectively.

✝

FEEDBACK
"This logo gives us the flexibility we need."

CAPITAL VIEW

Capital View offers viewing facilities for companies wanting to carry out market research and product tests, presenting products visually to focus groups and enabling discussion about them. The studios are based in central London and afford a stunning view over the British capital's skyline. So when it came to designing an identity for Capital View, Stereo decided to create a main logo that would suggest thought bubbles while also tracing London's skyline. The different colored circles of the logo are suggestive of the many different opinions being aired, say the designers. It is also a design that is very versatile and which allows the logo to adopt different forms, such as a speech bubble, or thought bubble. It is also a solution that would lend itself well to animation at a later point.

KULTUR.UNTERNEHMEN. DORTMUND

DESIGN *Martin Schonhoff and Michael Thiele, Die Transformer*
ANIMATION *Sebastian Rühl*

RULE 3... AND HOW TO BREAK IT!
A flexible "fillable" marque allows constituent parts to claim their own share of the logo, maintaining continuity while offering flexibility.

✝

FEEDBACK
"It's too complex and makes excessive demands for users in terms of the plurality of the logo."

"What kind of filling shall I pick now?"

MEMBERS OF KULTUR.UNTERNEHMEN.DORTMUND

To promote start-ups in design and other parts of the creative industries, the University of Dortmund, Germany runs an organization called kultur.unternehmen.dortmund (Cultural Enterprise Dortmund). It is part of a wider body that aims to promote business initiatives in the region known as G-DUR, for whom Die Transformer had designed a logo some years previously. For kultur.unternehmen.dortmund, the design consultancy decided on a radical solution that would have a logotype accompanied by a logo shape that could be adapted to each individual start-up. "The name remains—the icon changes. Its shape is an abstraction of the borders of Dortmund," explains Martin Schonhoff. "Metaphorically speaking, it provides a framework for any contestant or any possible creative discipline: photography, typography, writing, directing, painting ... you can even run animations or movie clips in it. The logo is live and very emotional." However, it was a solution that worried the client, who felt a logo should always be identical for maximum recognition and were concerned about responsibility for "corporate design mistakes" during realization. As a result, this design was abandoned in favor of a more conventional approach.

Go Local

DESIGN *Max Kaplun*

Go Local is an example of the increasing blurring of the lines between creating a campaign and developing an identity. Six separate logos, each with its own fluorescent color and handwritten treatment, and changing every week in the summer of 2008, were created by Max Kaplun for NYC & Company, the official body promoting New York. While its usual practice is to bring in tourism from outside, here the emphasis was on getting New Yorkers to explore their own city and perhaps discover new aspects of their hometown. "The logo had to convey an idea of urgency and took the form of a sticker being slapped over text," says Kaplun. "It was placed on bus shelters, handout cards, beach balls, frisbees, and stickers."

RULE 3... AND HOW TO BREAK IT!
In a campaign environment, changing the design week by week further assists the core task of getting people's attention.

⸸

FEEDBACK
The campaign was positively covered in both national and local media.

MIAMI ART MUSEUM

DESIGN *BaseNYC*

IMAGINE M!AM!

In advance of the opening of the new Herzog & de Meuron–designed Miami Art Museum in 2011, BaseNYC developed an identity for a capital campaign to raise funds. In some senses it's an identity that, while fresh, is traditional—the "i's" are inverted to form exclamation points, and the color refers to the seafront location and planting integral to the building. But other aspects are less conventional. "Rather than create a single logo for MAM's capital campaign, we designed a flexible system fusing visuals and written messages," BaseNYC explain. "Incorporating the distinctive aqua blue exclamation points into headlines such as 'Imagine!' and 'Envision!', the identity functions on multiple levels and creates a voice for the [campaign] rather than a static logo." And as the project and building evolve, so will the logo system designed to support it.

RULE 3... AND HOW TO BREAK IT!
By changing form, the identity can contribute to the moment in a campaign environment such as this.

BEAUT!FUL JO!N NOW!

Half Each

DESIGN *Stereo*

halfeach
halfeach

RULE 3... AND HOW TO BREAK IT!

There is a novel reason behind the variation in this logo design, which, while creating a talking point, is still closely tied with the overall branding of the company.

✝

FEEDBACK

"Our new identity really encompasses the direction in which our company is heading."

HALF EACH FOUNDERS

Half Each is a digital communications company that takes its name from the fact that its shares are owned equally by its two founders. The logo developed for them by Stereo is in some senses relatively conventional, with the two words separated or brought together by an invisible half line, enforcing the idea of sharing, not only between the founders, but also between the consultancy and its clients. One aspect, however, is unusual: the logo is seasonal and exists in two colorways. In the hotter part of the year, it is in two different shades of cool blue, "to chill you out," according to Matthew Simpson at Stereo. And in the cold months of winter, it adopts the warm red and orange hues of a fire to warm you up.

Open Intelligence Agency

DESIGN *Stefan G. Bucher,*
344 Design

RULE 3... AND HOW TO BREAK IT!
For a diverse and creative group
such as this, a multifarious identity
points to their strengths rather
than diluting them.

✠

FEEDBACK
*"I thought the planners might
want to scale it back, but they love
the squids and followed up with the
direction, 'More! More!'
They're cool people."*

STEFAN G. BUCHER, 344 DESIGN

Four advertising planners, in four different cities around the globe, comprise the Open Intelligence Agency. Pasadena-based Stefan G. Bucher was given an open brief to come up with a logo, and he responded with relish and humor. His solution was 12 different squid mascots, flexible enough to be played out in 48 design variations, and as comfortable on the web as tagged on a wall. "It was immediately clear to me that the Open Intelligence Agency is poised for world domination through brain power—much like giant squids, which are among the smartest animals on earth," quips Bucher. "I had also considered otters, but squids are more mysterious and look better as vector shapes."

DOG BLUE

DESIGN *Unit-Y*

Dog Blue is a dog sitting and care company based in Chicago. It approached Unit-Y to develop a "witty, unexpected, and standout identity." Andrey Nagorny of Unit-Y started off by creating a whimsical illustration of humorous interactions between man and dog. As this image progressed, it developed into a series of visuals, which he decided to refine and keep. "The end result was a series of three unique but visually unified logos, and a unified visual expression for the company," Nagorny says.

RULE 3... AND HOW TO BREAK IT!
Like frames from a cartoon, these images are unified rather than identical.

Stedelijk Museum CS

DESIGN *Experimental Jetset*

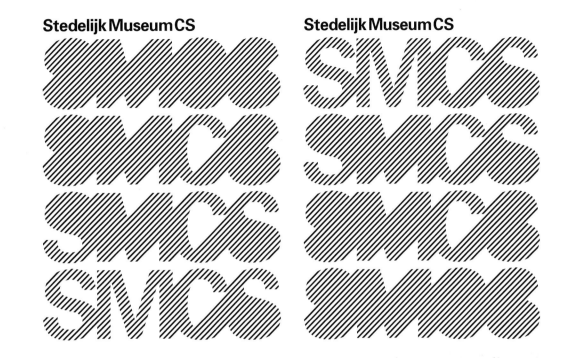

RULE 3... AND HOW TO BREAK IT!

If the organization the logo is for is in a state of flux, why not the logo too?

While its new home was being built, Amsterdam's Stedelijk Museum (City Museum) moved temporarily into an old building that had belonged to the Dutch Post Office. Only able to show some of its work, it was now known as the Stedelijk Museum CS, and a new identity was commissioned from famous local graphic design group Experimental Jetset. As the museum was in a state of transition, they wanted the logo to be in a state of flux too, so it exists in four variations. The use of the acronym SM and of the font Univers are both references to the work done for the institution in the 1970s by legendary Dutch graphic designer Wim Crouwel. The use of red and blue diagonal lines is a reference to the pattern found on airmail envelopes, in deference to its new home in what used to be the Post Office. Designing a logo for the new institution was a project close to the heart of Experimental Jetset, who felt it was a sort of homage to two historical social-democratic institutes from their youth.

Doodle4Google

DESIGN *Various designers*

WINNING ENTRY FOR THE USA IN 2008 BY GRACE MOON, A SIXTH GRADER AT CANYON MIDDLE SCHOOL, CASTRO VALLEY, CALIFORNIA. © GOOGLE INC. USED WITH PERMISSION.

RULE 3... AND HOW TO BREAK IT!
What better way to seem like a natural part of the landscape than to allow children to express temporary ownership of your brand?

✝

FEEDBACK
The Doodle 4 Google initiative regularly receives positive coverage by some of the biggest names in national and international media.

Most large corporations police their logo with military ruthlessness, but Google had the imagination and bravery to take a pioneering approach to flexible branding. The search engine's famously simple title page began carrying various small alterations to commemorate festivals or events or to share messages with its users. While some inside and outside Google thought that to meddle with its logo was commercial suicide, it has proved a very successful strategy for embedding the logo seamlessly into people's lives and evincing positive emotions. While most of the "doodles" as Google likes to call them are drawn by "master doodler" Dennis Hwang, Google has also begun to hold competitions around the world, inviting schoolchildren to create their own version of the Google logo, with the best appearing on the Google home page for a day to be seen by millions. Whether playful irreverence or the insidious creep of subliminal marketing into the schoolroom, the project shows that flexible branding can be every bit as powerful as the cookie cutter "Coca-Cola" alternative.

DOODLE BY SEAN STAATS, PADEN CITY ELEMENTARY,
WEST VIRGINIA.
© GOOGLE INC. USED WITH PERMISSION.

DOODLE BY HYLAND SLADE,
OLD DONATION CENTER, VIRGINIA.
© GOOGLE INC. USED WITH PERMISSION.

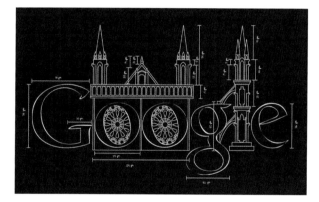

DOODLE BY PAUL MASSICOTT, HADDAM-
KILLINGWORTH HIGH SCHOOL, CONNECTICUT.
© GOOGLE INC. USED WITH PERMISSION.

DOODLE BY HANNA GOLDSTEIN, DEERFIELD
ELEMENTARY SCHOOL, NEW JERSEY.
© GOOGLE INC. USED WITH PERMISSION.

CENTQUATRE

DESIGN *Experimental Jetset*

RULE 3... AND HOW TO BREAK IT!

"It is perfectly acceptable that a person will first receive an invitation carrying a Medium logo, and a few weeks later an invitation carrying a Light logo. This 'instability' is to underline the idea of the 'work in progress.'"

THE 104 MANUAL

CENTQUATRE (104 in French) is the name of an ambitious cultural institute in Paris, France, providing a home for up to 30 artists at a time, of all kinds and from all over the world. Experimental Jetset, the Dutch graphic design group well known for its bold and innovative work, was approached to develop a logo and brand identity. "We want to present the graphic identity of 104 not as a set of laws, but as a graphic language. A language that contains, just as any other language, not only rules, but also a structure, a grammar, and most important of all, a certain spirit," Experimental Jetset explain in the very detailed book of instructions they drew up. The identity is seen as scaffolding built up from the logo which is essentially "a line, a circle, and a triangle," which approximate to the numbers 104. The logo and branding is designed to work in four different weights, which can be varied at will so that "the viewer will always be confronted with another version of the logo," reinforcing the sense of work in progress that is at the heart of the institute.

LE
104
CENT
QUATRE

LE
104
CENT
QUATRE

LE
104
CENT
QUATRE

CHAMBER MUSIC AUSTRALIA

ART DIRECTION *Andrew Ashton*
DESIGN *Marco Gjergja,*
Andrew Ashton
Studio Pip and Co.

RULE 3... AND HOW TO BREAK IT!
Variations on a theme, as
musicians know, are a good
way of maintaining interest.

Chamber Music Australia's main activities are international and national chamber music competitions. It approached Studio Pip and Co. to create an international brand for the cultural organization, something that would attract a younger audience, while at the same time maintain the support of the existing and older audience and appeal to government groups and sponsors. The solution was one that questioned existing rules and expectations of a single, fixed logo. It sought instead to replicate the intricate and varied experience of listening to music. "We developed a phonetic-type mark that remained unchanged, but that was juxtaposed with a range of abstract symbols that were devised to express the many moods and expressions found in chamber music," says Ashton.

The Parlour

DESIGN *Andrew Ashton,*
Studio Pip and Co.

RULE 3... AND HOW TO BREAK IT!
Be greedy—have a few different logos
and use them all at once.

The Parlour is a hairdressing salon based in the lively Melbourne suburb of St. Kilda, which wanted an adventurous identity to reflect its "wayward and diverse customer base." What it got, rather than a single logotype, was a variety of different and contrasting logos that are to be piled up and superimposed upon each other in different ways—a concept that works as well in print as animated on the salon's website. "An individual and their hair is a unique expression, and we wanted to reflect that in a typemark that has varying yet familiar outcomes," says Andrew Ashton.

K2 Screen

DESIGN *SEA Design*

RULE 3... AND HOW TO BREAK IT!
Reflect the client's business by creating something bespoke each time.

✝

FEEDBACK
Job bags, posters, and business cards bearing the logo have become collectible items.

K2 Screen is a small screen-printing company in London that does high-end work for a variety of designers and publishers. It approached SEA Design, one of its clients, looking for a logo that would show off the process of screen printing as much as was possible. The result is an interlocking logotype that changes color and position with each application. Rather than being a single, consistent memorable image, with a fixed position and color, what you remember is the process, or a certain kind of look. Suggestive of a process, it was a solution that readily lent itself to animation for K2's website.

SAKS FIFTH AVENUE

ART DIRECTION *Michael Bierut*
DESIGN *Jennifer Kinon*
and Kerrie Powell
Pentagram

RULE 3... AND HOW TO BREAK IT!
"The advantage of the program, deployed in black and white, is that it creates recognizable consistency without sameness."
Michael Bierut, Pentagram

✝

FEEDBACK
"The updated logo gives us a modern look that is sure to resonate with our customers and contribute to the resurgence of Saks Fifth Avenue."

STEVE SADOVE, CEO, SAKS INCORPORATED

Saks Fifth Avenue is one of the most iconic retailers in the world, with a logo drawn by design legend Massimo Vignelli in an ornate cursive style in the 1970s. Updating the logo without junking its heritage wasn't an easy task for Pentagram's Michael Bierut, who had himself worked for Vignelli. So Bierut and his team took the existing logo, redrew it, and placed it in a black square, which was then subdivided into a grid of some 64 smaller squares, each containing a chunk of the logo. "The 64 tiles can then be shuffled or rotated to form an almost infinite number of variations," he explains. "The individual logo tiles are interesting in their own right, and within the system can be used to form still more abstract compositions. Each of these suggests within its details the graphic character of the new logo." Another virtue of the new logo system is its versatility for the many applications required, including packaging, signage, direct mail, and advertising.

A&P BY...

DESIGN *Various designers*

RULE 3... AND HOW TO BREAK IT!
Make the logo a destination,
something you relish like a visit
to a buffet rather than something
you just record subliminally in passing.

Every time you go to the website of Accept & Proceed, a London-based design and art direction consultancy, you see a different logo created by a different designer or illustrator. "Creatives of all disciplines have been asked to create an A&P logo for the company," the founder David Johnston explains on the site. "Aside from using only black/white/grayscale and representing an A&P in some way, there is no brief, allowing contributors to work as they do best, uninhibited by direction and creating work for the love of it." The project is open and ongoing, and over 100 creatives have submitted A&P logos in a bewildering variety of forms.

THOU SHALT MAKE A MARQUE THAT IS CONSTANT AND UNCHANGING

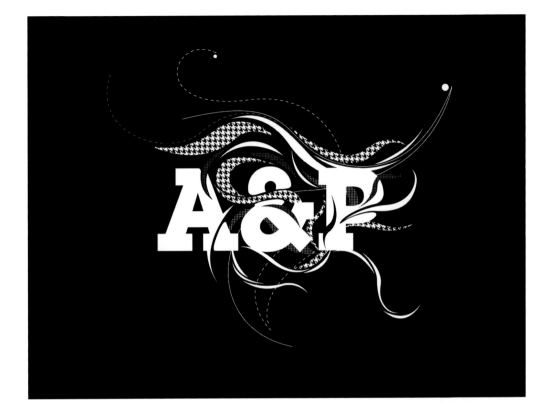

119   NO RULES LOGOS

P.O.V.

ART DIRECTION *Paula Scher*
DESIGN *Julia Hoffmann*
Pentagram

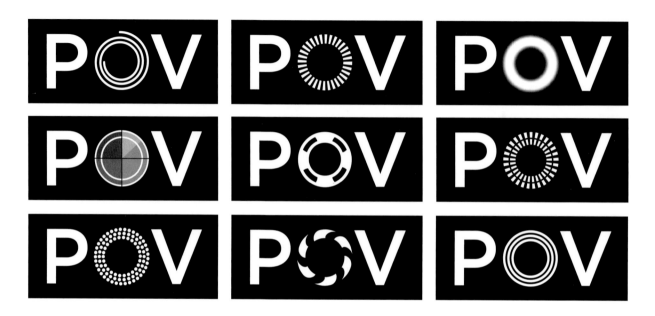

RULE 3... AND HOW TO BREAK IT!

A flexible and fluid logo form can only reinforce the message that this is a series that presents different points of view.

P.O.V. is a documentary film series on US public broadcasting channel, PBS. It presents stories and issues that are otherwise neglected, hence the name P.O.V., a cinematic term for "point of view." Pentagram devised a logo for a series that would also project a point of view, allowing the logo to change according to nine different standardized patterns. While the logo is a simple affair set in Gotham, the "o" changes—so it can be a playful spiral, a film about children, or an ornamental pattern for a historical documentary. For motion graphics, posters, and advertising print campaigns, the "o's" are filled with stills from specific films in the series. "P.O.V. is about individual points of view. Changing the 'o's' allows the identity to customize itself," says Julia Hoffmann, who designed the logo as part of Paula Scher's team at Pentagram's New York offices.

SYMPTOMS

DESIGN *MWM Graphics*

RULE 3... AND HOW TO BREAK IT!

If you are wearing a logo on your chest, you might care more about visual interest than marketing.

Among other things, the Symptoms Collective sells T-shirts made from a combination of hemp and organic cotton. These feature the word "Symptoms" on the front in designs by MWM Graphics, the working name of Matt W. Moore. It is then a Symptoms logo, but not *the* Symptoms logo. As such its attitude and visual play is of more importance than its legibility, and this logo itself has spawned a number of variations.

PERSONA

DESIGN *MWM Graphics*

RULE 3... AND HOW TO BREAK IT!

Why have one logo when you
can have many?

For Persona, a boutique retailer of T-shirts, MWM Graphics created not one
logotype, but a whole series, a sort of equivalent to the musical variations
on a theme. One logo, the one featuring a dollar sign, was used for signage,
while the others, all in contrasting styles, were used on T-shirts.

PURE GROOVE

DESIGN *Patrick Duffy, No Days Off*

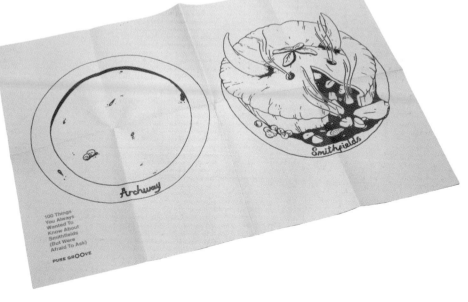

Pure Groove is a long-established London record store that has grown bigger and bigger over the years, branching out to running its own label and small-scale publishing business, as well as holding exhibitions. It approached local design consultancy No Days Off looking for a new brand identity that would be flexible and able to evolve over time. Patrick Duffy created a solution that is both typographic and pictorial: while most of the logo remains steady, the two enlarged "O's" are open to separate interpretation, changing and developing with the particular application and time.

RULE 3... AND HOW TO BREAK IT!
One way of making sure your logo doesn't date is to design it with the door open to future developments.

MTV Idents

ART DIRECTION *MTV Networks*
ILLUSTRATION *Serge Seidlitz*

Moving logos that pop up regularly between TV shows need to entertain, be fun, and bring a smile to your face, however many times they're viewed. For MTV's Emerging Markets channel rebrand, Serge Seidlitz was asked to create a movable feast, an overflowing vocabulary of images, some in color, some in black and white, some animated, others static. Together they create an identity. Seidlitz also progressed the MTV tradition of differently colored logos. And by grafting his strange creatures directly onto the main MTV logo, he also demarcated certain programming, tastes, and trends in music, with additions such as a hip-hop ball-cap wearing logo, and the axe-wielding, heavy metal guitar-hero logo.

RULE 3... AND HOW TO BREAK IT!
Investigate the fun possibilities of setting up subbrands to add personality and to more closely target a very diverse audience in a highly competitive market.

NATIONAL DESIGN CENTRE

ART DIRECTION *Andrew Ashton*
DESIGN *Marco Gjergja and Andrew Ashton*
Studio Pip and Co.

RULE 3... AND HOW TO BREAK IT!
What could be more appropriate for a design center than something that requires continual design?

Based in Melbourne, Australia and funded privately, the National Design Centre is dedicated to design of all disciplines. It needed to establish an international brand to attract a broad audience, maintain the support of the design sector, and develop an identity that appealed to government groups and sponsors. "We found it difficult to capture this broad expression that is inclusive of all design practitioners and their work," says Andrew Ashton of Studio Pip and Co., which designed the branding. "It required a brand that represents all concepts, styles, trends, and processes of the design sector. Inspired by [conceptual artist] Sol LeWitt, we devised a design framework and instructions allowing every person in contact with the brand to generate an individual and unique symbol for the Centre. On a five by five matrix the individual brand designer is tasked to cast a mark, or draw, with any material, five lines that connect with points on the grid; the marks must touch all four outer edges of the matrix. A custom typeface was developed to express the main brand and subbrand associated with the Centre—called unofficially Fluffy Bold, or NDC Bold."

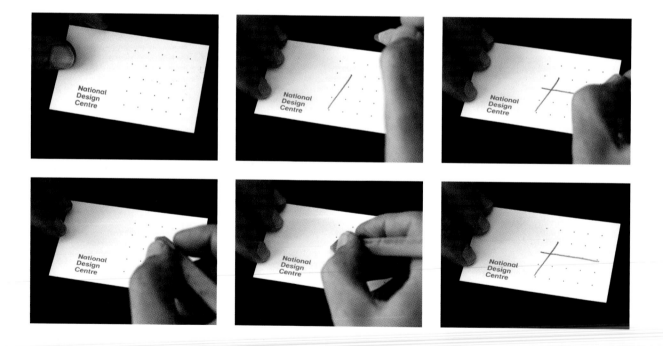

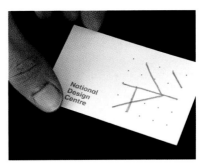

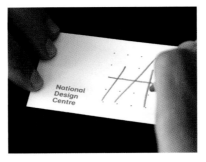

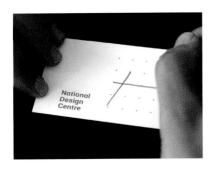

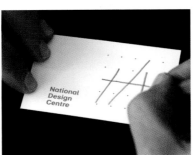

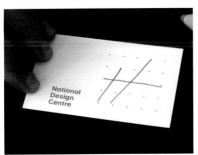

Rule 4

Simplicity is often seen as a virtue, particularly when it comes to logos. These, convention has it, should be as concise as possible, and easy enough to reproduce and use at different sizes without difficulty. But intricate, complicated logos can be terribly alluring.

THOU sHAlt keep it SImpLe.

ODECEIXE SURF CLUB

DESIGN *Samuel Nunes*

RULE 4... AND HOW TO BREAK IT!
If a logo is distinctive enough, it doesn't matter if people can read it easily or not.

✢

FEEDBACK
"People love using things with the octopus logo."
SAMUEL NUNES

On the beautiful coast line of Portugal's Algarve, you find the town of Odeceixe, popular with surfers wanting to take advantage of the Atlantic's swells and surf. The area is a designated nature park, and the Odeceixe Surf Club has the twin duties of looking after the local environment as well as fostering sustainable development of surfing.

So the theme of nature had to be present in the logo that Samuel Nunes was asked to design, but it was stipulated that the identity should also be "irreverent, daring, different." Nunes' unusual solution was to draw an octopus surfing, and using a mussel rather than a surfboard to do so. If this image required some deciphering, so did the accompanying typography. It is heavily condensed, the letters are of different sizes, and the overall logo is as full of swirly shapes as the sea itself. Naturally, the approach has lent itself to merchandising and other brand communications with ease.

PELIFICS

DESIGN *Eirik Seu Stokkmo, Teipu*

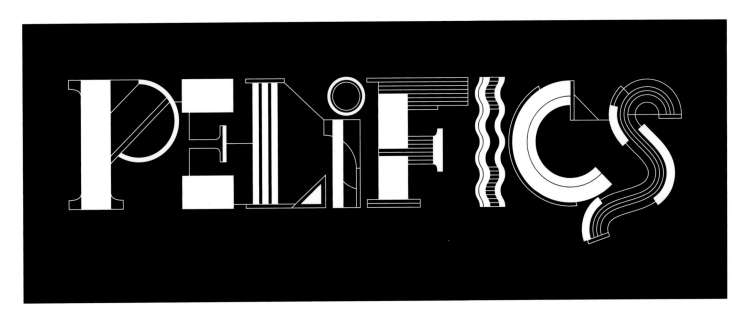

RULE 4... AND HOW TO BREAK IT!

If you're really trying to be pretentious, why create a logo that can be small and hide its light under a bushel?

As well as being a graphic designer, Eirik Seu Stokkmo is also a musician, and wanted to create a logo for himself that was as inspired by the 1980s as his music was. "Instead of opting for the more usual retro script, the inspiration is from the more pretentious and baroque side of 1980s art and typography," he says. "The logo becomes just as much an illustration as anything else, and can be used for a number of different purposes. Its sheer complexity and amount of detail means it will always have to be reproduced in larger sizes."

UNFOLDING TERRAIN

DESIGN *Francheska Guerrero,*
Unfolding Terrain

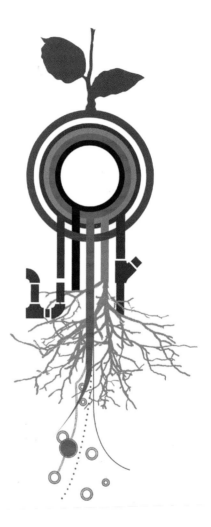

RULE 4... AND HOW TO BREAK IT!
An intricate design immediately
telegraphs the fact you are not dealing
with a stuffy corporate entity.

When Francheska Guerrero thought about the name and logo for her own graphic design practice, she developed an almost botanical concept that would suggest new growth and experimental space. "I researched numerous icons which could represent creative growth, both literal icons like plant life, and nonliteral abstract forms like op-art seeds and plumbing fixtures," she says. "I also wanted the color and forms to represent multiplicity."

The result was a logo that intentionally breaks the rules. "This logo design is not in the modernist tradition of 'timeless,' 'simple,' or 'universal,'" says Guerrero. "This is a complex logo with multiple layers of meaning, very fine line art, and numerous colors. The logo is used with and without text. The goal was to move beyond the conventions of current and historical logo design of simple mark-making reductivism."

She points out that with current technologies, such as the web and digital PDFs, it is now possible to create "more complex logos which technically work very well with web color space and full color possibilities with PDFs." She also notes that the current life span of branding and identity programs is much shorter than in earlier times when some of the most famous logos were developed. "Today, in our hyper image-saturated subcultural markets, we continually seek the next 'fresh thing,'" she says. "The universal audience no longer exists, we function in target demographics, and our logos—our identities—do not need to be watered down or become generic trademarks for mass consumption."

✝

FEEDBACK
"When I give people my business card, I get very good responses. Most people tell me the logo is very different–in a good way."

FRANCHESKA GUERRERO, UNFOLDING TERRAIN

Schouwburg Arnhem (Theater Arnhem)

DESIGN *Robert Overweg,*
Roberts Empire

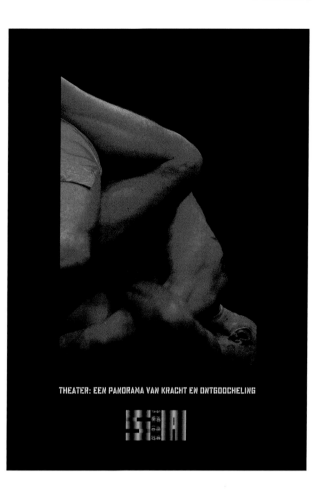

RULE 4... AND HOW TO BREAK IT!
A stark and provocative design sets out the uncompromising ambitions of the theater, which itself is happy to delve into complicated territory.

While still a third year student at the Arnhem Academy of Art and Design, Robert Overweg created a speculative logo for the local theater. Its unusual form is the result of Overweg taking the Photoshop swatch, cutting it up, and then putting it back together to create type forms. The result is a complicated, shimmering logo, and something that Overweg says looks a little "modern and mysterious for the likes of a theater" and "breaks with simple vector illustration style." It is certainly a logo that eschews the usual clichés of the theater.

The logo, together with a sample poster, was presented to the theater, which liked the logo and noted its potential for animation in online applications. However, as the theater had recently commissioned another logo, this one was left in the designer's portfolio.

TOTTENHAM

DESIGN *Belinda Hubball,*
Lloyd Northover

RULE 4... AND HOW TO BREAK IT!
Be greedy and let the logo demand
a little bit of space to breathe.

✠

FEEDBACK
"As Tottenham's image improves,
the area's excellent location, transport
connections, and below average
property prices will certainly place
[it] in a very competitive position
as a national and international
business location."

ANGIE CHANDLER, HARINGEY CITY GROWTH
BOARD MEMBER

Tottenham, in north London, has long been blighted by associations with poverty and crime. To spearhead an initiative to revive the area, a logo was commissioned from Lloyd Northover to shift the perceptions both of its residents and those outside the area. "Recent investment and development have transformed [Tottenham]. A new brand was needed to communicate and promote change," say the designers. The resultant "rallying call" was an intricate logo, made up of many little logos and well-known, evocative icons, all grouped into the shape of the letter "T" and intended to communicate Tottenham's "vibrancy." As well as blue, the official logo palette includes pink, orange, and lime. In tone, it is more akin to fashion branding, and the logo requires a reasonable reproduction size for its various elements to be discernible.

BARBRA STREISAND
2007 MINI TOUR

DESIGN *Ian Lynam*

When Tokyo-based Ian Lynam was asked by music merchandising agency Signatures Network to come up with a logo for a mini tour by Barbra Streisand, it was a commission that was particularly gratifying. "I grew up with my mom listening to Streisand's records, and due to that I have an appreciation for her music," he explains. "I wanted to create something for her that was atypical, stylish, and simultaneously something that both she and I would like."

The resulting logo is a monogram of the letter "B," made up of organic, botanic swirls that are ornate enough to make a viewer stop and think before the singer's initial becomes apparent. It's a logo that trades softness and intricacy for traditional ease of reproducibility and legibility.

RULE 4... AND HOW TO BREAK IT!
When the personality is as well known as this, a fair amount of divergence from the conventional can easily be carried—even if it does make life hard for printers.

CLINT LUTES

DESIGN *Amy Stafford, Studio Blixa 6*

RULE 4... AND HOW TO BREAK IT!
For a personal identity, standout and originality can be more important than clarity or ease of reproduction.

✝

FEEDBACK
The cards have had to be reprinted repeatedly because of their popularity.

Clint Lutes is an American dancer resident in Berlin, Germany. As well as performing himself, he is busy as a choreographer and teacher, stages a contemporary dance series called Lucky Trimmer, and has appeared on German television's *Stars Auf Eis* (Stars on Ice).

Capturing such a versatile personality was a challenge for designer Amy Stafford, a fellow Berlin-based American. She was asked to come up with a logo and tagline that would capture the full range of Lutes' personality and activities for use on business cards and other promotional items. Her solution is based on a photo she took of a pug called Hank, and ignores logo-making propriety by mixing raster and vector files, combining different genres, and by generally being complicated and messy. And to top it all, the idea came to her in a dream.

"I mentioned my dream [to Clint] and how I was thinking of using a pug dog as a mascot for him," says Stafford. "Surprisingly, he replied that he too had had a dream the night before about dogs, but had worried that I was going to choose a Jack Russell. He loved the pug idea though, so I ran with it and incorporated some 'champion-ish' oriented motifs. The solid process colors were inspired by childhood memories of old bubblegum wrappers and circus graphics."

LHHMA
(Lithuanian Hip Hop Music Awards)

DESIGN *Gediminas Siaulys, PetPunk*

RULE 4... AND HOW TO BREAK IT!
Given the limited use and applications of this logo, an interesting feel was more important than any consideration of practicality.

When Lithuanian artist and designer Gediminas Siaulys was asked to come up with a logo for a local hip hop music awards event, he decided to take an approach that would avoid the obvious. "The aim was to create a logo for the local viewer, with a Lithuanian attitude to hip hop," he explains. "I wanted it to have a different feel from American hip hop culture, so no 'gangsters and bling-bling.' The idea was to be true to ourselves."

If the logo breaks with the rules of what hip hop graphics should look like, so does it break the rules of what a logo should be. Siaulys freely admits it is not scalable, and would be totally unreadable if printed small. It also breaks with convention in using photographs of tape rather than type for all the words bar one, and that is seemingly hewn from out-of-focus wood. It is urban and gritty, but in an unexpected way.

AGDA (Australian Graphic Design Association)

ART DIRECTION *Shane Keane, Anthony DeLeo, and Scott Carslake*
DESIGN *Shane Keane*
Voice

RULE 4... AND HOW TO BREAK IT!
There is probably no group more used to pared-down minimalism than graphic designers, so keeping things busy is a good way of attracting their attention.

✠

FEEDBACK
"We had plenty of positive feedback from a critical audience of graphic designers, and at least one irate letter to the editor in the daily newspaper from an offended local."
SHANE KEANE, VOICE

Design consultancy Voice was asked to come up with an identity for the Ninth AGDA National Biennial Awards and Conference in 2008 that was held in its home city of Adelaide. The idea was that the identity would play its part in enticing graphic designers from around the country to come to Adelaide for the four-day event. Voice decided to create a logo that would take a bunch of (sometimes offensive) stereotypes about the city, such as being known for "bizarre murders, weirdos, churches, and a large lesbian population," and play with them to create an unusually busy and old-fashioned logo. "Instead of dismissing these opinions, they are embraced to create a fun and quirky characterization of the city," says Shane Keane of Voice. "The promotional material that accompanied the identity used a wide range of visual styles and themes. The identity took from all these elements and mashed it into one big flamboyant logo."

The resulting deliberate "hotchpotch" seems more like a nineteenth-century gun brand than a twenty-first century grouping of graphic designers, until you look closely as its constituent images, which include Chihuahuas and churches. It was used both in black and in white when against a colored background.

WIDAMON MÁTÉ

DESIGN *David Barath*

RULE 4... AND HOW TO BREAK IT!
To be distinctive, decorative, and topical here is more important than the need to impart information quickly.

Widamon Máté is a cinematographer based in Budapest, Hungary. He wanted a logo that he could use for his personal communications, DVDs, and website, and when he approached fellow Budapest resident David Barath, the only stipulation was that he wanted it to be a playful engagement with his initials. "I realized that the letters M and W are the reflections of each other," explains Barath. "All I did was simplify them to the minimum and use some wit with the act of 'cut.' I have replaced the initials with basic geometrical forms and, by placing them one after the other, created a rhythm that is decorative in itself. If used on a black background, this logo evokes the pattern of the 'cut' clapper board, which signals 'start working' for cameramen."

Hungary is the only country in Europe to use the "eastern" order of names, so the surname is placed first. But here, given that the logo takes as its starting pointing the fact that the letters M and W are mirror images of each other, the order becomes irrelevant as it can work equally well each way.

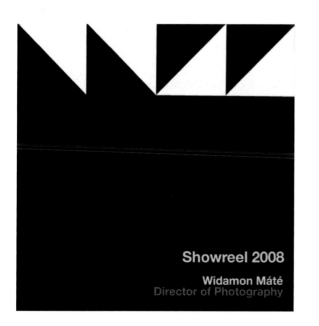

Showreel 2008
Widamon Máté
Director of Photography

CIRCUS SCIENCE

ART DIRECTION *Hans Allemann*
DESIGN *Gergory Paone and*
Hans Allemann
Paone Design Associates

Circus Science was an exhibition held at The Franklin Institute Science Museum in Philadelphia, which sought to engage visitors with scientific principles through metaphors and themes drawn from the world of the circus. The museum wanted a logo that would have general appeal beyond the core audience of children, and that would also work on stationery and marketing materials, as well as an animation presented in a kiosk at the start of the exhibition. Paone Design took the invitation to create a playful identity to heart, and developed what they call a "highly illustrative letterform design, with a complex color arrangement and a genuine avant-garde spirit of discovery." As it had to work across various platforms, the logo was developed to work in one, two, and three color forms.

RULE 4... AND HOW TO BREAK IT!
Sometimes, it's a case of the busier, the merrier.

✛

FEEDBACK
"The logo was very well received not only by children but also by adults attending the exhibition. Local media and sponsors embraced the mark, reportedly due to its energy and child-like qualities."
GREGORY PAONE, PAONE DESIGN ASSOCIATES

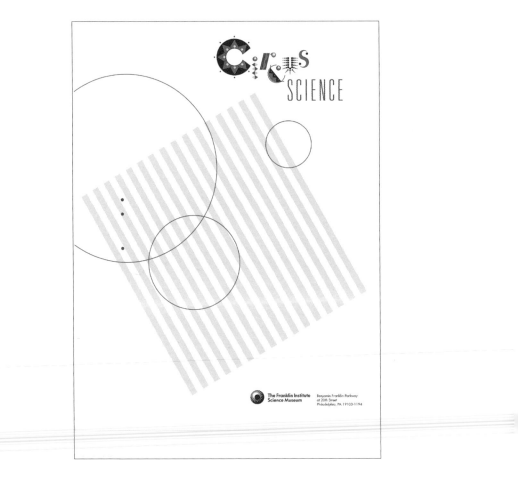

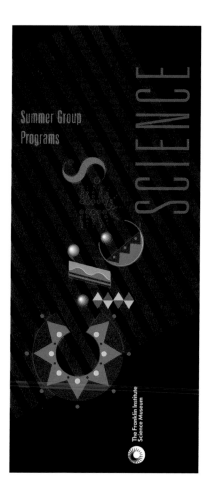

Circus Science

June 11 – September 6
Mondays – Sundays, 9:30 a.m. – 5:00 p.m.

CIRCUS SCIENCE is your chance to run away and join the circus. The show starts in the Benjamin Franklin National Memorial with a thrilling aerial/juggling performance, moves to the Midway to look at the science behind the circus and then to special workshops. This event was developed in cooperation with Ringling Bros. and Barnum & Bailey Circus.

Workshops: Juggling, Magic and Clowning!

Mondays, Tuesdays and Wednesdays 11:00 a.m.
Duration: 45 minutes
Cost: $2.00 per person
Capacity: 30

In these special, hands-on workshops, you can clown around, juggle with the best of them, and pull the wool over people's eyes using your amazing magical skills.

Junior Clown College
Your chance to create your own clown persona! Learn about the history of clowning, and discover the art of putting on your own clown face. (Ages 6 & up.)

Mastering the Art of Magic
Discover the importance of hand-eye coordination, and learn the science of optical illusions. (Ages 8 & up.)

Give and Take Juggling
Have a blast learning the fundamentals of physics – like Newton's laws of motion and the effects of gravity – in this step-by-step approach to juggling. (Ages 8 & up.)

COME AND CELEBRATE THE 200TH ANNIVERSARY OF CIRCUSES IN AMERICA AT THE FRANKLIN INSTITUTE AS IT HOSTS THE SHOW OF ALL SHOWS... CIRCUS SCIENCE. IT'S A LITTLE BIT OF HISTORY, A GENEROUS DOSE OF NOSTALGIA, AND SOME REVEALING SCIENTIFIC INSIGHTS INTO WHAT MAKES THOSE AMAZING CIRCUS FEATS POSSIBLE.

STRAIGHTLINE

DESIGN *Khaki Creative*

RULE 4... AND HOW TO BREAK IT!
Rather than being impossible to print small, have a logo that changes according to its size.

Straightline is a business consultancy that facilitates contacts between companies in the West with companies in China. "Straightline, 'Zhi Xian,' refers to the Chinese concept of the best, fastest, and most direct way to achieve your objectives," its website announces, and this is something that was picked up literally in its logos, one in Chinese, the other in English. "We used straight lines all linked together to design this English font. In terms of the Chinese font, we similarly used this method of linking straight lines, though the result was much more coarse," explain Khaki Creative. While accepting that logos usually need to be able to be printed quite small, the level of detail present in these logos would be lost. However, this achieves an optical effect—the straight lines of the bespoke type seem to be curved when printed small enough.

LITTLE HERO

DESIGN *Rick Milovanovic, Alter...*

LITTLE HERO

RULE 4... AND HOW TO BREAK IT!
To suggest humility and simplicity in an original way, paradoxically this logo had in some technical ways to become rather complicated.

✝

FEEDBACK
"The client is very happy with this logo. We think it really sums up the idea that anybody can be a hero on a small scale."

RICK MILOVANOVIC, ALTER...

Rae Begley runs a small PR agency in Sydney, Australia, focusing on local rather than international work, something encapsulated in her company's name—Little Hero. She approached design agency Alter... looking for a logo that would be "fun, playful, and personal" while also being professional. The designers explored the notion of "being a hero on a really small scale," or someone who is "proud of their achievements in a really humble way." The unexpected end result is, they playfully suggest, either "a podium with no one standing on it, or a wooden Tetris piece." A hand-drawn scrawl, gradually getting smaller, functions as the logotype. But the designers are proud of their little design and its rule breaking: "Logos are generally clean, scalable vector shapes with solid color. The Little Hero logo is a raster image, it's small and doesn't scale to grand sizes very well," they say.

LUCKY COQ

DESIGN *Jonathan Wallace, Alter...*

RULE 4... AND HOW TO BREAK IT!
To achieve the handcrafted, distressed quality desired, any notion of keeping things uncomplicated had to be thrown out the window.

✠

FEEDBACK
"Wow that is a beautiful rooster, why does my computer crash when I open the EPS file?"

MAX FINK, LUCKY COQ

Lucky Coq is a pizza joint and bar located in the Windsor suburb of Melbourne, Australia. The brief to local graphic designers Alter... was to come up with an "illustrative logo that has an antique or historical character." Something, in other words, that would match the relaxed retro charm of the venue and its vintage furniture. Drawing very loosely on cigarette branding, Jonathan Wallace developed a process color (four color) detailed illustration of a rooster, accompanied by retro typography. "We drew plenty of roosters and had to decide how to combine this with period typography in a sympathetic way," says Wallace. "The result was something that is modeled on wartime aircraft painting."

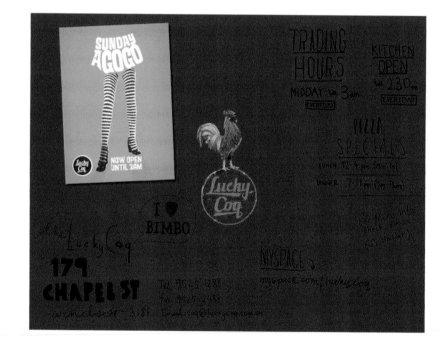

Waterform Design Inc.

DESIGN *Masayo Nai, Waterform Design Inc.*

RULE 4... AND HOW TO BREAK IT!
Once the narrative is followed and decoded, the core attributes of the company will have pressed themselves forcibly on the viewer.

✝

FEEDBACK
"It's been well received so we decided to make more promotional pieces using the logo."

MASAYO NAI, WATERFORM DESIGN INC.

When Masayo Nai designed a logo for her own design consultancy, Waterform Design Inc. in New York, she wanted something that would demonstrate creativity and hard work, yet still be fun. Into the melting pot went a series of images of everyday items, including a pencil, a chicken, an egg, and a crank, and from these a light-hearted, cartoon-like mark was created. Humor and narrative were prioritized over simplicity and accessibility. Unusually the logo tells a little story of a chicken laying an egg. It's metaphorical yet presented in greater detail than would normally be found on a logo. When printed, the logo is produced with a matte, silver foil stamp to "give a modern industrial feeling."

DAILY MONSTER

DESIGN *Stefan G. Bucher,*
344 Design

RULE 4... AND HOW TO BREAK IT!

When you're doing your own thing,
rules don't really matter.

DailyMonster.com is the blog of designer Stefan G. Bucher. For this website, which he describes as an "online drawing and storytelling experiment," he wanted to devise a logo that would "communicate the open and friendly 'made by humans' spirit and invite people to participate." The end result was a complicated, hand-drawn lockup which includes the logo as well as other bits and pieces. "After fiddling with a very clean vector logo for a while, a friend pointed out that the site is all about making things by hand. After that, it all fell into place," Bucher recalls.

SKIN Aesthetic Medical Clinic

ART DIRECTION *Katrin Olina Petursdottir*

DESIGN *Siggi Orri Thorhannesson and Sól Hrafnsdóttir, Grafiksense*

RULE 4... AND HOW TO BREAK IT!

The delicate filigree suggests something premium and feminine, but its straightforward base means legibility isn't compromised.

✠

FEEDBACK

Winner of the 2008 Iceland Graphic Design Association's award for identity design.

Located in a palazzo near the Ponte Vecchio in Florence, Italy, the SKIN Aesthetic Medical Clinic offers a variety of cosmetic surgeries and treatments in a lush interior designed by Michael Young and Katrin Olina Petursdottir. Its modern yet very feminine interior is permeated by floral decoration. After completing the interior, Petursdottir invited fellow Icelandic graphic designers Grafiksense to design an identity for the clinic, something that would be strong yet make clear reference to the clinic's interior design. Their solution has a straightforward basis of a sans-serif type that however seemingly dissolves into flowers that echo Petursdottir's wall decoration for the clinic. As well as being used for all its communications, the logo features on the clinic's bespoke door handles.

Zwols Studenten Cabaret Festival

DESIGN *Kim Smits and Matthijs Maat, MAKI*

RULE 4... AND HOW TO BREAK IT!

Increasing recognition and standout can be achieved by making a logo that is complicated and long as well as short and snappy.

✝

FEEDBACK
"It's got us lots of new jobs."
MAKI

Zwolle is a city in the northern part of the Netherlands, which holds an annual student cabaret festival. As is often the case with these events, the logo, accompanying posters, and other materials have to work together as a package. Rather than come up with a snappy name for the festival, MAKI kept its full excessive length for the logo and came up with a snappy creature instead. "For some reason, we often end up using an animal in our logos. In this case, the alligator had the right character. With its huge smile that could eat you up or make you laugh, it was perfect for the cabaret festival," say the designers.

The long name of the event is further complicated by hand-drawn, cloud-like letterforms, either in white against a busy background so the name stands out and can be seen at a distance, or set in a variety of colors emanating from the alligator's jaws in other applications.

Rule 5

IF THERE IS ANYWHERE YOU DON'T WANT TO MAKE A
MISTAKE, SPELLING OR OTHERWISE, IT IS IN YOUR LOGO.
BUT SOMETHING THAT SEEMS TO BE AN ERROR CAN ALSO
BE A SURE WAY TO GRAB ATTENTION.

Thou shalt not maKe mistakes

Clubcollective

DESIGN *Bunch Design*

club collllective

club collllective
www.clubcollective.com

club collllective™
www.clubcollective.com

RULE 5... AND HOW TO BREAK IT!

A deliberate misspelling allows an otherwise simple logo to come to life and creates an additional element that can have its own identity.

Clubcollective is a multilingual online portal featuring nightclubs across Europe. Given the many languages the portal is available in (in addition to English, it features Catalan, Spanish, Dutch, French, German, Italian, Greek, and Czech) a certain freedom in the spelling of the word "collective" is perhaps less of an issue than it otherwise would be. For in the logo that Bunch Design came up with, the double "l" in the word collective becomes a quintuplet "l," in different heights, as if it were an electronic display of music on a mixing desk. As such the grouped letter "l's," all at different heights, can be detached to become a logo in their own right. When detached, they are given a varied and colorful treatment. The relatively sober logo contrasts well with the more informal style of the rest of the portal's communications.

HOTEL MORE

DESIGN *Boris Ljubicic,*
Studio International

m o o
oooo
oore

RULE 5... AND HOW TO BREAK IT!

Opening a word up with repetitions in a way that challenges standard spellings is a risky business, but can convey a playful confidence.

✠

FEEDBACK

The logo was initially accepted by the client, but was then rejected for fear that the logo would suggest an unintentional spelling mistake had been made. It has been replaced with an innocuous and generic swirl.

The luxurious, five-star Hotel More is located just outside the beautiful, historic city of Dubrovnik on Croatia's Adriatic coast. Its name "More" is a bilingual pun—in Croatian it means "sea" whereas in English it means "abundance." Asked to develop a visual identity for the hotel that would encapsulate the beauty of its surroundings and its luxurious facilities, Boris Ljubicic came up with a bold, punning, typographical design that played with both meanings of the hotel's name. To suggest abundance, the amount of "O's" in the name More could be extended indefinitely. "The languages [English and Croatian] are equalized by a witty design," suggests Ljubicic. "The number of letter 'O's' changes and therefore the logo is unstable and nonidentical in its various applications. Yet the design uses simple typography [the font De Vine in italic and normal]." It was, however, an approach that proved too radical for the client, who eventually rejected the design.

THEORETICAL GIRL

DESIGN *Nick Cannons Studio*

Theoretical girl

RULE 5... AND HOW TO BREAK IT!

To leave out a letter from a word is unusual, but to omit the initial letter from a name in a logo is courting trouble. But the logo remains just about decipherable and is intimately tied to the image of the singer herself.

Theoretical Girl, aka Amy Turnnidge, is a UK-based indie singer with a quirky style, mixing 1960s girl-band sounds with an art deco look and existential lyrics. The singer-songwriter, signed to Salvia/XL, needed a logo that could be used for all her promotional materials. Nick Cannons came up with something as quirky as the singer herself. "The customized font uses sharp, heavy shapes that don't really sit on any particular line, but are contained enough so that they don't seem to float, and the tracking is all over the place," explains Cannons. "We were trying to reflect the 'lo-fi' appeal of the music. Some recordings were quite raw, which led to the jagged shapes."

But one feature of the singer influenced the logo very literally—her haircut. Instead of the letter "T" at the start of the logo, you find the Theoretical Girl's distinctive, jet-black 1930s bob depicted. Nevertheless somehow the logo remains legible. And its heavy distinctive messiness allows it to stand out on sleeve cover artwork.

Zero

DESIGN *Andrey Nagorny, Unit-Y*

RULE 5... AND HOW TO BREAK IT!

The unexpected placement of the square as the letter O (and its pun on the number zero) reinforce the intellectual aspirations of the music group the logo is for.

"Zero is a Chicago-based music band known for its experimental, minimalist approach to music. The band blends various electronic styles with more traditional eastern music," explains Andrey Nagorny of Unit-Y, a graphic design company also based in Chicago which was asked to come up with a visual identity. To be in keeping with the band's ethos, the logo would have to be "simple, but sophisticated and visually impactful."

Nagorny chose to go for a purely typographic solution. "To create a visual impact through typography, an unexpected placement of the letter O was used. This creates a memorable visual expression which allows the letter O to be read as a letter and also as a number 0," he explains. But, of course, rather than a circular letter or number form, it is actually a square.

CHEW IT OVER

DESIGN *Stereo*

RULE 5… AND HOW TO BREAK IT!
Given that these school materials were designed to encourage debate, having elements in the logo that seem unusual or wrong can pique curiosity and encourage critical reflection.

London-based consultancy Stereo was asked to come up with an identity for an educational program called Chew it Over, together with accompanying materials, for chewing gum brand Wrigley's. "The logotype has been created with a bespoke 'friendly' font and with differently colored speech bubbles, depending on the text," says Matthew Simpson at Stereo. As the project was intended to stimulate discussion in the classroom, transforming the dot above the "i" into a speech bubble gave the logo flexibility—not only could it vary in color with the topic, but it could also be used in the design to incorporate other elements, such as headlines and so on. The letter "e" was also inverted, as if in reflection, and the font generally undermined the spelling.

ANDREW PEGLER
MEDIA

DESIGN *Andrew Ashton,*
Studio Pip and Co.

RULE 5... AND HOW TO BREAK IT!
The shock of seeing mistakes and
their correction, shows people how
important copy-editing is.

Andrew Pegler Media is a copywriting and editing company based in
Melbourne, Australia. It wanted an identity that would captures its clients'
imagination and highlight the difference that quality, plain English copy
and editing can bring to the communication process. "[Andrew Pegler
Media's] service is often about taking an existing text and filtering it
with a professional copywriter and editor's experience and insights,"
explains designer Andrew Ashton of Studio Pip and Co. "We felt that this
identity could be a process and that this process could be conducted in
the customer's presence." So rather than a slick, fixed logo, there is an
assemblage of copy that needs to be separately edited and corrected with
the superimposition of a red pen.

Timebased

DESIGN *Steve Payne, Studio Output*

RULE 5... AND HOW TO BREAK IT!
The unusual use of seemingly incorrect punctuation functions as a point of interest and encourages the viewer to delve deeper into the rationale for the name.

Timebased is an events company based in London with a client list that includes upmarket brands such as Harrods, Laurent Perrier, and *GQ*. To maintain its own image in a very competitive market, it wanted a new logo that would reflect the kind of high-end events it organizes. On the one hand, the logo is very simply constructed with a sans serif, but the details challenge. It breaks the company name into two, stressing the element of time that is at the heart of what Timebased does, and then adds what looks like incorrect punctuation. But instead of speech marks, the inverted commas instead refer to the symbols for a minute and a second.

Fwend

DESIGN *Andrew Black, Blackbooks*

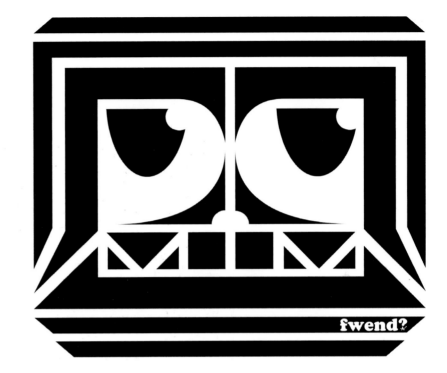

RULE 5... AND HOW TO BREAK IT!
When a logo is as weird as this, deliberate misspelling doesn't seem such a big deal.

To drum up interest in their design studio, Blackbooks, Andrew Black and BOOKSIIII decided to created a branding campaign that would use a different, and rather weird, logo. While suggesting a book in two halves, it also has a curious, cutesy misspelling of the word "friend." "Fwend was originally designed for Blackbooks as a sticker to get up in the streets," says BOOKSIIII. "Then it was transferred over to advertising to introduce our company to new clientele and get them to sign up for our mailing list."

Rule 6

Unconventional logos, in all their shapes and sizes, show how many other ways there are of sticking your tongue out at logo propriety. Here's a gallery of rogues, breaking some of the less known logo sins.

Thou shalt not create a rogue

Central Films

DESIGN *Zoveck Studio*

THOU SHALT NOT USE COLLAGE

..AND HOW TO BREAK IT!

Collage is not usually a technique used for logos, but here it allows a retro image to be used in a way that is modern yet witty.

✝

FEEDBACK

"The logo was very well received, and the company now uses it for all its communications. They've also made T-shirts, notebooks, publicity, and so on using it."

ZOVECK STUDIO

Mexican film company Central Films decided it needed a new look and asked Zovek Studio to develop a new logotype. "There were really no concrete restrictions or specifications. The company just wanted a modern and playful logo that would help them stand out from the competition," says Julio Carrasco of Mexico City-based Zoveck Studio. The brief simply was to create a logo that would indicate that the company films all sorts of things all over the world. "The main idea was to change Central Films' old concept of a train station to that of an intelligence agency or a detective agency, very similar to that of Agent 86 in the 1970s TV series *Get Smart*. We took inspiration from *Get Smart*'s gadgets with double functions, such as the Shoe Phone and the Cone of Silence. Since Central Films has many prestigious directors, we decided to turn it into a place full of secret agents that go on the most complex of missions anywhere in the world." By using montage, Carrasco developed a logo that suggested the world of film in a humorous and memorable way.

Dag van de Architectuur Groningen (Groningen Day of Architecture)

DESIGN *Kim Smits and Matthijs Maat, MAKI*

THOU SHALT NOT HAVE AN ARBITRARY WORD BREAK

... AND HOW TO BREAK IT!

With a logo as wacky as this, chopping up the word "architectuur" (architecture) only adds to its naïve appeal.

✝

FEEDBACK
"It went done well as it appealed to both the traditional architecture crowd as well as young people interested in the event."
MAKI

The city of Groningen in the Netherlands holds an annual day of architecture (Dag van de Architectuur Groningen), and each year the event is given a different visual identity. For 2008, local design consultancy MAKI came up with a rather rude little logo. It sticks its tongue out at convention by not only having a line break, but also ragged edges to its typography. To that you can add its use of negative space, and just to increase the fun, the logo is animated on the event's website to flash in a series of three garish colors.

The brief was simple: the logo had to link to the subject matter in hand—buildings, that is—and appeal to a wide cross section of people beyond the architectural cognoscenti. Its primary application was to be on flyers and posters for the event, where it becomes the predominant feature. Indeed, the logo feels like an extrapolation from the poster rather than the other way around. The designers arrived at the shape by playing around with the patterns created by skylines and cityscapes. The resultant evocative shape then had the name of the event spelled out in letters messily cut out of it.

HJÄRTA SMÄRTA

DESIGN *Hjärta Smärta*

**THOU SHALT NOT HAVE A LOGO MADE
FROM NEON LIGHTS
..AND HOW TO BREAK IT!**
Neon lights are often used for store
signs, and in some ways this designer's
logo is that too, proclaiming their
individuality and creativity rather than
any particular wares.

Designing your own logo means you have the perfect client, or at least, one that gives you plenty of freedom. So when Stockholm-based duo Angela Tillman Sperandio and Samira Bouabana went about designing a logo for their own graphic design consultancy, they were able to be a bit more experimental than would otherwise have been the case. Interpreting the idea of a shop sign in a literal yet radical way, the pair used fragments of neon—broken up and discarded elements of other signs—to create their new logo. "We liked the idea of working with a material which had already been used by someone else," they explain. "The neon has to be recycled in some way so we used it to build a new sign—our logotype. And because the logotype is built up by pieces of other signs, the final design is partially random." It has also been the departure point for a personal project of neon signs that the pair mix with their commercial work.

La Redonda

DESIGN *Zoveck Studio*

THOU SHALT NOT USE PHOTOGRAPHY IN THINE LOGO

... AND HOW TO BREAK IT!

Mixing photography and hand-drawn type with more than a nod to religious iconography results in a complicated yet distinctive and versatile logo.

✝

FEEDBACK

"The logo was used the entire time the show was on the air, and some animations were made of it to be shown during the breaks."

ZOVECK STUDIO

La Redonda is an irreverent television show about soccer, presented by two musicians and a model, rather than the usual lineup of players, ex-players, and pundits. The show needed a logo that would be similarly unconventional. Given complete creative freedom by the clients, Pepe Carmona and Alejandro Abramovich at MTV Latinoamérica, Zoveck Studio came up with a kitschy, playful, and rather ornate logotype. "Since the show was not presented by soccer professionals, we decided that the fun and nonprofessional way to play this sport was table soccer at the fair," says Julio Carrasco. The designers chose a figurine, clutching a ball under his arm, to represent a table soccer game. Rather than drawing this figure, as would normally be done for a logo, they decided to photograph it in a lurid viridian. This photograph then formed the heart of the identity.

NEXT COFFEE COMPANY

DESIGN *Bryan D. Hughes, assisted by Floyd Orfield and Daniel Jaramillo, NextStudent Inc.*

THOU SHALT NOT STAIN THINE LOGO
... AND HOW TO BREAK IT!
Photograph a splodge and dislodge preconceptions of what a coffee logo should be. Nescafé, Starbucks, and Illy, for example, may have some of the most memorable and distinctive logos out there, and you are unlikely to beat them at their own game, so why not try something completely different?

✝

FEEDBACK
"It captures the casual, light atmosphere of the place."
COMMENT REPORTED BY THE CLIENT

"I wanted to break away from the stylizations of beans, coffee cups, and so forth that dominated the results of my research," says Bryan D. Hughes, tasked with developing an identity for the Next Coffee Company. "Using photographic elements in a logo is a pretty big no-no, but the image of a coffee ring left after a satisfying cup of coffee was just too good to pass up. Five pads of differently textured paper and a full pot of spilled coffee later, I had the perfect shape."

"Although photographic, [the logo] works great as a two-color screen, and prints perfectly in all those places a photographic element just isn't supposed to. To me, this is an example of how breaking some rules doesn't have to result in a complicated or hard-to-use logo."

The Cheshire Dental Clinic

DESIGN *Matthew Miles, Jordangate*

DR HELEN MITCHELL BDS
SURGICAL DENTIST

**THOU SHALT REFER TO THE COMPANY
AND CREATE A LOGO, RATHER THAN
USING RAMBLING PHOTOS
... AND HOW TO BREAK IT!**

A small dental practice is a very
different entity to a global packaged
goods company, and conveying the
correct impression here is more
important than cementing recognition
of a name.

A dental practice located in the north of England wanted a logo that would
convey both a friendly image and a sense of clinical expertise. Matthew
Miles' solution is not so much a logo in the conventional sense of a graphic
device as a corporate "image." In the place of the company name, there is
a photograph of the dentists themselves, with their white coats rendered
from white space. "The archetypical image of friendliness is a smiling face,"
says Miles. It is a solution that, while unusual and ingenious, lends itself
easily to the various kinds of communications issued by a dental practice.

FEEDBACK
*"The feedback has been mixed–the solution was
unexpected and therefore quite challenging."*
MATTHEW MILES, JORDANGATE

COMMAND+N

DESIGN *Apirat Infahsaeng*

The artists' collective, Command+N, is made up of graduates of the University of Connecticut, where designer Apirat Infahsaeng had himself studied. Infahsaeng came up with an identity for the collective that is so way-out it hardly seems fitting to call it a logo.

"I was interested in creating typography that relied on the presence of color for legibility," explains Infahsaeng, whose day job is as a senior designer at BIG, part of Ogilvy & Mather, New York. He readily accepts he ignored the idea that a logo should be "a pared-down and simple form." "I treated this as more of a painting," he says.

THOU SHALT KEEP TO PRIMARY COLORS OR BLACK AND WHITE ... AND HOW TO BREAK IT!
Not every logo needs to be printed on bottle tops, and while this may present printers with a few heart-stopping moments, it is eminently suitable for an artists' collective.

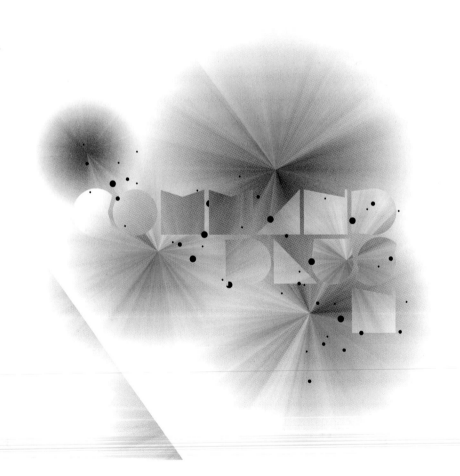

JOURNEYS FOR CHANGE

DESIGN *Ulhas Moses, UMS Design*

Journeys for Change is an initiative from "social entrepreneurs" UnLtd, a charity based in the UK that takes influential people on trips to different parts of the world to interact and learn from different cultures and mindsets. The first trip was to India, and Mumbai-based designer Ulhas Moses was briefed to come up with a logo that reflected "that life-changing transformation that can take place in an individual after such an experience."

Moses decided to use the metaphor of the butterfly to suggest both travel and transformation from "a raw state into something truly different and beautiful" for the logo he developed. "The logo had to reflect the energy and enthusiasm of the journeys, and that sense of excitement has been used to create the logo itself," he recalls. "So, no computers, no straight lines."

The actual logo was arrived at by simply splashing acrylic paint to form the butterfly's wings, and the name of the organization was set at an angle for further dynamism. For its application on stationery, a further element was added—by means of a simple die cut, the wings of the logo's butterfly were lifted as if it were about to flutter off.

THOU SHALT NOT USE DIE CUT

... AND HOW TO BREAK IT!

Die cuts may be impractical for most applications, but here, for a small print run, it fits nicely with the design.

✝

FEEDBACK
The client loved the rawness and spontaneity of the logo.

Kaj Runelund – Varumärkesrelationer

DESIGN *Henrik Persson, Become*

THOU SHALT NOT MIX DIFFERENT LANGUAGES ... AND HOW TO BREAK IT!

To have two different symbolic fields in operation—logotype and txt language—would normally invite confusion, but here there is a very clear justification for doing so.

Kaj Runelund is a Swedish marketing consultant and wanted a logo for the company he runs under the title of Kaj Runelund – Varumärkesrelationer (which translates as brand relations). His philosophy is based on a mix of psychology and marketing, believing that "an organization's wellbeing is in direct relation to the quality of the last meeting, either between employees or between the company and client or customer." It's an approach he sums up with the slogan: When I am OK, and when you are OK—then we can meet.

"Known as being different, funny, precise, and inspiring, he also wanted to tie in the concept of brand relations and 'human meeting' in the logotype," says Henrik Persson, of Stockholm-based design consultancy Become. His solution to this was to introduce mobile phone "txt" speak and the emoticons of internet chat to the logo. The end result uses the symbol for two "kissing smilies" as the representation of Runelund's theory of both sides being happy. It is a very personal logotype that takes risks by drawing on another symbolic language.

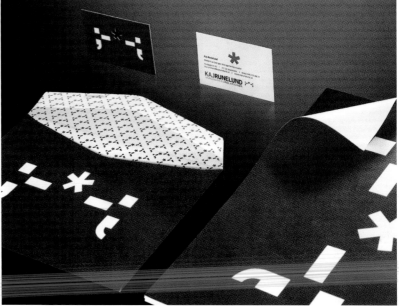

BIMBO DELUXE

DESIGN *Jonathan Wallace and Dan Whitford, Alter...*

Bimbo Deluxe is a bohemian yet rustic pizza restaurant in the fashionable suburb of Fitzroy in Melbourne, Australia, that transforms itself into a trendy bar at night. Its owner, Max Fink, wanted a logo with a "cheeky, slightly disturbing edge," and graphic designers Alter... were happy to oblige. "A process of happy accidents developed through various illustrative experiments until we found something that could be reproduced across various media and gave some sense of curiosity," explains designer Jonathan Wallace. The result was an illustration, in two Pantone colors, based on a Kewpie, the doll-based magazine character that first appeared in the Ladies' Home Journal in 1909. It is an eccentric image that gives a distinctive flavor in its many applications.

**THOU SHALT NOT DRAW DOLLS
AND CALL THEM A LOGO
... AND HOW TO BREAK IT!**
An existing character, given a new treatment, takes on a quirky life of its own.

✝

FEEDBACK
"The client has used this motif ad infinitum, and we have had many really interesting and creative briefs as a result."
JONATHAN WALLACE, ALTER...

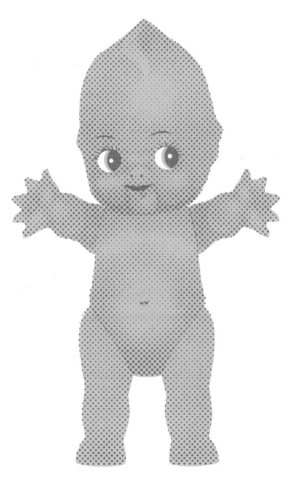

Meme for Adam et Ropé

DESIGN *Lee Basford, Fluid Design*

**THOU SHALT NOT PRODUCE
SCULPTURE AND CALL IT A LOGO
... AND HOW TO BREAK IT!**

This is branding at its most literal—
except, rather than a red hot cattle
branding iron, one of the exhibits acted
to offer the imprint. In a society where
the woodprint is deeply culturally
ingrained, it is an appropriate yet
novel approach.

Japanese fashion brand Adam et Ropé held a series of exhibitions in
its Tokyo store around the idea of "memes," that is, cultural events that
operate almost as viruses. *Homme Meme* was the punning name of the
show, and Lee Basford, an art director at Fluid Design, an advertising and
design consultancy in Birmingham, UK, contributed a logo. This had to
be adaptable to a variety of applications including merchandise, but also
had to "encompass elements of artistic originality."

Basford's day job at Fluid involves hours spent at his computer working
digitally, so to compensate, he produces sculptural works hewn from wood
in his spare time. This gave him the idea to create a logo that was primarily
three-dimensional—essentially sculptural typography chopped out of
wood. As building blocks, the wooden type forms echoed the memes that
formed the inspiration of the exhibition.

A wood print was made from them, which was then scanned to form
the basis of the logo which was used for all the printed communications.
"From its origins in wood, the logo breaks rules from the outset in that
the materials dictated the outcome to a large extent, rather than a specific
typeface or traditional way of creating a logo," says Basford.

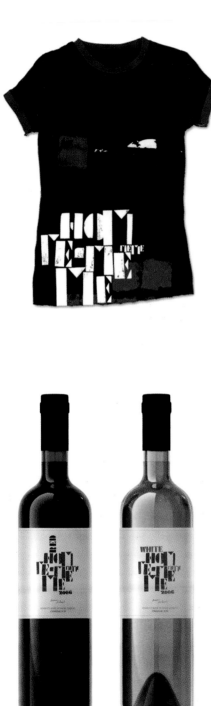

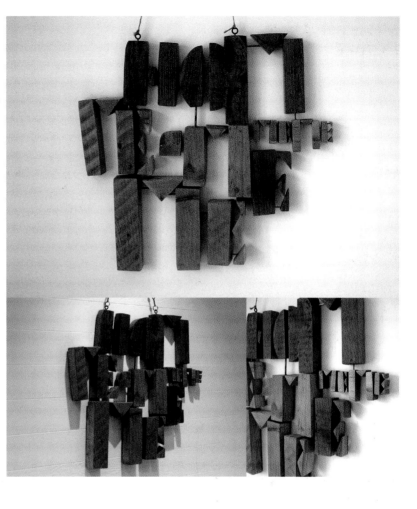

✚

FEEDBACK

The wooden sculpture/sign that was the logo's archetype
remained as a feature in Adam et Ropé's flagship store in
Tokyo well after the end of the exhibition.

GIRLS ROCK!

ILLUSTRATION *Melina Rodrigo*
DESIGN *Joshua Berger, Plazm*

Girls Rock Productions - 588 Guerrero Street
San Francisco CA 94110 - tel: 415-517-1979
info@girlsrockmovie.com
www.girlsrockmovie.com

THOU SHALT NOT SCRIBBLE

... AND HOW TO BREAK IT!

Given the limited application of the logo, creating impact and expressing the movie's attitude were more important than any other consideration.

✠

FEEDBACK

"The client was happy with the outcome and the documentary was picked up by a distributor, screened at film festivals and theaters around the world, and is being prepared for international DVD release."

JOSHUA BERGER, PLAZM

Aimed at challenging stereotypes, *Girl's Rock: The Movie* is a low-budget independent movie that documents the experiences of four girls between the ages of eight and 18 attending the Rock 'n' Roll Camp for Girls. The production company needed a logo so that the film could be packaged and effectively marketed to potential distributors. The logo had to capture the energy and independent spirit of the movie, and make a similarly challenging statement. Plazm, based in Portland, Oregon, was approached to come up with a design, and their response sought to encapsulate the "independence and ferocity of spirit, coupled with a heavy dose of rock 'n' roll and DIY attitude" of the movie. "Melina Rodrigo drew, painted, wrote, and scrawled the title of the film dozens of times. These were combined and layered into the final word mark for the movie," explains Plazm's Sarah Gottesdiener.

Plastik

DESIGN *Stereo*

THOU SHALT ONLY USE
ONE OR TWO FONTS
... AND HOW TO BREAK IT!
Using different typefaces for each
letter allows the individual letters to
have their own life and suggests a
collection of objects, reinforcing the
name of the club night.

For a club night in London called Plastik, promoted by entertainment
company Luminar, design consultancy Stereo created a simple yet very
distinctive logo. Typographic convention usually requires that logotypes
use one, sometimes two, fonts. But here each letter of the name was
assigned a different and unusual font. "This gives the feeling of being
plastic, almost as if different objects had been brought together," says
Stereo's Matt Simpson.

✝

FEEDBACK
"It's a very strong and original marque that
represents our club night perfectly."
DHILON SOLANKI, CAMPAIGN MANAGER, LUMINAR

Sally's Place

ART DIRECTION *Adam Wahler*
DESIGN *Max Kaplun*

**THOU SHALT NOT PUT HOLES
IN STATIONERY
... AND HOW TO BREAK IT!**
Milking the iconography of records
allowed for an innovative if somewhat
impractical approach.

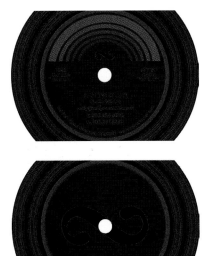

Adam Wahler runs a printing business and is a frequent customer at Sally's Place, a folk and jazz record store in Conneticut that has a cult following. Thinking the store would make a nice project, he took it upon himself to team together with designer friend Max Kaplun to develop a new identity system for it. What they came up with is a curved shape that suggests both musical notation and the "S" from the name of the store's proprietor, Sally White. This design could be used flexibly on everything from the storefront, to records, business cards, stationery, and advertising. Elements from records, such as a central hole and a round shape, were transferred to business cards and stationery for an unusual yet highly recognizable effect. Max Kaplun describes this as the "most clever and reserved" of the solutions developed, but sadly it wasn't implemented. "Sally loved the identity, but changing the identity of the store, or adopting an identity wasn't her thing," says Kaplun. "She's into music, not brand identity."

FIAT

DESIGN *RobilantAssociati/Fiat Centro Stile*

THOU SHALT NOT KEEP ON CHANGING THINE LOGO

... AND HOW TO BREAK IT!

Rebranding to draw a line under recent difficulties is not unheard of with consumer brands, so why not in the automotive sector?

✠

FEEDBACK

"We have decided to acknowledge the progress achieved so far by changing our logo as a tangible sign of the new impetus that is projecting us towards future challenges."

LUCA DE MEO, PRESIDENT OF FIAT BRAND

Car marques account for some of the most enduring, distinctive, and prized logos ever created. Logos such as BMW's propeller or the three-pointed star of Mercedes are classics that are instantly recognizable anywhere in the world, and apart from minor tweaks and tucks have changed very little in over a century. While other, less classic, car marques have needed more plastic surgery over time, continuity is still the byword. However, Italian manufacturer Fiat has taken a much more modern, cavalier approach to its logo, changing it quite drastically and quite frequently by industry standards. From the late 1960s, it had a clean modernist logo with the four, italicized letters split by slashes against a blue background. But by 1999 this had been junked in favor of a reinterpretation of the 1920s logo, also against a blue background, until in 2006 this logo was revisited again. Redrawn and now against a red background, the logo has lost the laurel leaves on its external circle. It will no doubt be tweaked again in the future.

Sideshow

ART DIRECTION *Stefan Sagmeister*
DESIGN *Stefan Sagmeister, Kiyoka Katahira, Matthias Ernstberger, Sarah Noellenheidt*
Sagmeister Inc.

Sideshow Creative, a production company with bases in New York, Los Angeles, and London, needed a new identity to mark important strategic changes to the company. It approached Stefan Sagmeister looking for a logo that would above all stress the flexibility and creativity that Sideshow Creative wanted to project. The result was a corporate identity that split Sideshow into its constituent two words: side and show. These two words were placed in a sequence in which one morphed into the other. Business cards presented the changeover by lenticular means, allowing the letter I to become H, and E to become W when tilted.

THOU SHALT NOT BREAK ALL THE RULES AT ONCE

... AND HOW TO BREAK IT!

Lack of constancy and legibility, as well as dissecting the company name, do not prevent this logo from standing out and signaling its intent very forcefully.

✝

FEEDBACK

"Hiring such creatives took us to a whole new level that we would not have reached on our own. We have been very happy with the results."

MIKE MCCALL, PRESIDENT OF SIDESHOW CREATIVE

DOROTHY GOODBODY

DESIGN *Matthew Stuart*

THOU SHALT NOT BE SEXIST

... AND HOW TO BREAK IT!

If your target audience is middle-aged men, give them what they want.

✠

FEEDBACK

"The Independent Complaints Panel accepted that the image was slightly saucy, but in the style of an old-fashioned seaside postcard. Overall, the Panel decided that because this is just a drawing rather than a real woman, and the sexual connotations are so mild, the drink is not in breach of our Code."

PORTMAN CHIEF EXECUTIVE DAVID POLEY

The Wye Valley Brewery is a small family concern in Hereford, in England's rural hinterland. Despite its recent establishment, it trades heavily on its traditional brewing methods, including that of its Dorothy Goodbody line of beers. The lightly redrawn logo for Dorothy Goodbody stout, showing a Marilyn Monroe-like figure, hiking her legs up to show a glimpse of underwear, caused controversy and a formal complaint from the charity Alcohol Concern that it broke UK alcohol marketing guidelines by associating drinking with sexual satisfaction. The complaint was however rejected by governing bodies. The brewery said the logo was merely a fun image "conjuring up the spirit of 1950s Herefordshire." Marketing for the beer included news clippings pretending to be from the 1950s with various double entendres such as "Enter Dorothy Goodbody," applying the risqué element already present in the brand name and image.

RMN (Réunion des Musées Nationaux)

DESIGN *Experimental Jetset*

THOU SHALT NOT CHOP AND SLICE EXISTING LOGOS

... AND HOW TO BREAK IT!

Redesigns usually start afresh, but here a continuity is preserved without creating a hotchpotch of conflicting styles.

Réunion des Musées Nationaux is an umbrella organization for 35 museums dotted around France. Its original logo—a black circle, containing a white letter "M"—was designed in 1969 by Adrian Frutiger, before a tweak in 1990 (by Jean Widmer) saw the words "Réunion des Musées Nationaux" added to the circle. But in 2006, it approached Amsterdam-based graphic designers Experimental Jetset to redesign their logo so the emphasis would be on the acronym RMN, rather than on the single M, or on the full name. "The solution came to us quite quickly," the designers say. "It was obvious to us that the original logo, the circled M, already contained, within itself, the two letters needed to complete the RMN acronym. So we cut the old logo in half, liberating the R and N, and placed them alongside the M, thus completing the full acronym. The old logo looked quite static, as the dynamism of the slanted M was completely neutralized by the circle. By adding the diagonal slashes, the logo becomes dynamic again: it suddenly gets a rhythm, a movement."

Sansaw

DESIGN *SEA Design*

Sansaw
Modern
Rural
Living

THOU SHALT NOT INCLUDE

INTRICATE FOLIAGE

... AND HOW TO BREAK IT!

For a client keen to show the world it
is taking a different line, a large and
intricate logo helps make the point.

Sansaw is a modern English country estate with organic farms and rare breeds of livestock. SEA Design was asked to devise a logo that would encapsulate its tag, "modern rural living." Mixing serif and sans serif type, and varying in color, the mainstay of the logo is however a pictogram that shows the filigree of tree branches in a reverse silhouette, appearing like tiny veins. The very delicacy and fineness of the image requires the main decorated "S" to be of a certain size in order not to be lost.

AIRSIDE

DESIGN *Airside*

The first rule break on this project was for a design consultancy to redesign its own logo, something normally seen as an admission of weakness. But Airside, well known for its colorful and humorous approach to design, had the confidence to reevaluate its logo as part of its 10th birthday. To reflect the direction the consultancy was now heading in, the new logo had to work well both in still and animated form. "The result was a logotype whose individual characters seem frozen in a moment of movement," the designers explain. "It is a logo that moves without moving, while the accompanying set of animations build upon the movements suggested by the static mark." To make sure this approach would work, Airside designed a bespoke typeface, so that the letterforms would from the very start carry the group's stamp. The logo's frozen movement allowed the creation of what Airside calls "a family of sliced logos" to be used for different applications such as DVD covers. The group's previous business cards had been very well received as they carried a vector portrait of the carrier, but these needed to be rethought for the new brand. The result was a wavy line which when turned on its side forms the profile of the person whose card it belongs to.

THOU SHALT NOT SLICE BITS OUT OF THINE LOGO

... AND HOW TO BREAK IT!

Chopping the logo up gives you lots to play with, while also suggesting movement without resorting to cliché.

Airside

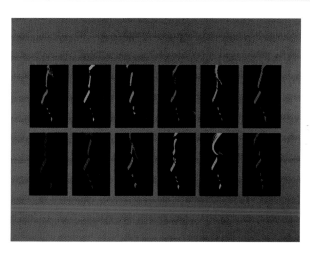

DREAM RANCH

DESIGN *Airside*

THOU SHALT MAKE THINE MIND UP
... AND HOW TO BREAK IT!

Perhaps the most difficult thing to do with a logo is to give the final yes, particularly if you have a set of strong rival contenders.

Dream Ranch was an agency representing artists in Japan. Part of its stable were well known UK design and illustration consultancy Airside, who felt that the existing logo was in dire need of a revamp. At first, one particular logo was preferred which, say Airside, "takes the name of the company and turns it into something from which objects are flowing. This flow represents the movement of ideas and creativity in the nature of the company." While initially favored for its playfulness and predisposition to animation, a more traditional logo was then favored featuring a cockerel, before the future of the company was thrown into doubt. If the company were to get a new lease of life, this would be the choice, but if minds were changed again, there would be a nice selection to choose from.

Dream Ranch

Dream.Ranch

Dream Ranch

Dream Ranch™

HOLLY SHIT

DESIGN *Dušan Jelesijević*

THOU SHALT NOT SWEAR
... AND HOW TO BREAK IT!

When an organization is all about giving society the finger, logographic propriety is pretty meaningless.

✝

F E E D B A C K

"I got a job offer from the Far East to be a lead graphic designer in an advertising agency, but when they asked me about this logo they took it as ridicule to their faith. So I didn't get the job despite not being a full-time member of Holly Shit."

Dušan Jelesijević

Holly Shit is a small group of people who support the underground scene in Serbia. "They organize concerts, exhibitions, drunken nights, parties, conferences, sport tournaments and shows, fooling-arounds—all imbued with punk-rock attitudes and influences," explains Dušan Jelesijević. "The name was chosen in opposition to traditional Serbian society, which is dealing with 'childish' problems in the twenty-first century, problems solved by other countries many decades ago." The fingers in the logo represent two letters from Serbia's Cyrillic alphabet: the letter "X" is the same as the Latin "H" and letter "Ш" is the equivalent of the Latin "SH." It is sarcastically presented in an official selection of color variations.

Edith Bowman

ART DIRECTION *Ross Stirling
and Dom Williams*
DESIGN *Ross Stirling
Studio Juice*

**WHEN CREATING A LOGO FOR AN
INDIVIDUAL, THOU SHALT INCLUDE
THEIR NAME
... AND HOW TO BREAK IT!**
When the client's name is
well known, let them function
as a visual marque instead.

Just draw the client. That was the solution adopted by Studio Juice when developing a logo and stationery for the UK television presenter and BBC Radio 1 DJ Edith Bowman. Rather than a traditional logo, the client's face forms the basis of an illustrative stencil. The approach is purely iconic—it doesn't use words or the client's name. "It represents the client directly through a raw yet feminine design," says Dom Williams. The logo features as a graphic stencil on Edith Bowman's home page.

BASTARDGRAPHICS

DESIGN *Julien Rivoire,*
Bastardgraphics

THOU SHALT CREATE A LOGO

NOT A PATTERN

... AND HOW TO BREAK IT!

Loosen up and rely on something
other than an icon or logotype to
give you a visual identity.

✠

F E E D B A C K
My clients seem to love it.

JULIEN RIVOIRE, BASTARDGRAPHICS

Julien Rivoire, an illustrator and designer based in the French city of Lyon, wanted to revamp his website and create new business cards, but didn't really need a logo in the conventional sense. Instead, what he produced for Bastardgraphics, the name of his consultancy, is an experimental and decorative pattern that can be used for his communications in a loose, yet distinctive way. "This is a pattern, so it can work everywhere. It could be used for an allover T-shirt, [it] could be on a wall, [it could] be used for a carpet, or anything else," says Rivoire. "I added a bubble with the word 'Hi!' because I thought that was quite funny."

Den Haag (The Hague)

DESIGN *Anton Corbijn*

THOU SHALT NOT SPRAWL

... AND HOW TO BREAK IT!

If convention has it that logos should sit meekly in the corner, then this one is greedy for space and clamors for attention, and controversy is rarely a bad thing when you are trying to raise your profile.

✝

F E E D B A C K

The logo perplexed other designers and was greeted with scandalized fury by the burghers of The Hague.

Anton Corbijn, the Dutch photographer and movie director, is best known for his feature films and collaborations with bands such as Joy Division and Depeche Mode. Given his background, it's perhaps unsurprising that the logo he has designed for the city of Den Haag (known as The Hague in English) is, well, a bit unusual. A very freely drawn kite with something that could be the "h" of Den Haag/The Hague on it, it mixes the styles of Joan Miró and Piet Mondrian in a way that confounds convention. It's a sprawling shape that requires plenty of space to work. The Hague in the Netherlands is best known as the home of the International Criminal Court, and this logo is part of a city marketing initiative to draw attention to its other attractions including art galleries and beaches. It was launched with lavish celebrations at the end of 2006, led by the proud Mayor who hoped the mark would become so well known and identified with the city, that the words Den Haag (or The Hague or La Haye) could be dropped from the logo in the future. An accompanying musical logo was later commissioned from Robert Jan Stips.

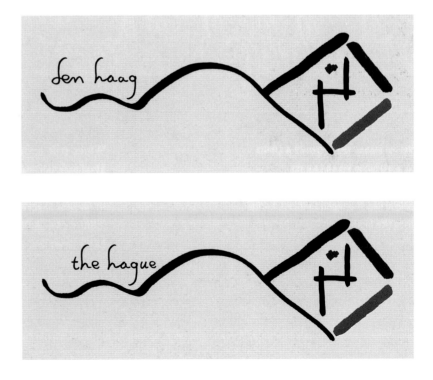

Sprjomi

DESIGN *Sól Hrafnsdóttir*

THOU SHALT NOT SQUIRT A LOGO

... AND HOW TO BREAK IT!

Despite the technical complexity, being
literal has managed to inject humor
into the logo.

While still a student at the Iceland Academy of the Arts in 2005, Sól
Hrafnsdóttir designed a logo for Sprjomi, which is an abbreviation of
"sprauturjomi," Icelandic for canned whipped cream. The execution is
both literal and intricate, seemingly created out of the squirting of cream
from a can. A full typeface was developed in support, which also seems to
be entirely written in cream.

ART OF MOVIN BUTTS

DESIGN *Blackbooks*

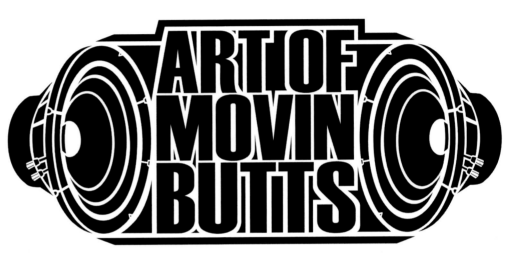

THOU SHALT NOT USE RUDE WORDS

... AND HOW TO BREAK IT!

Use enough craft and you will
be forgiven.

BOOKSIIII of Blackbooks created a signature stencil for the Art of Moving Butts, a monthly underground hip-hop night in Miami, staged by Counterpoint Garments' Paul "Gnu" Jennings. A cheeky use of the word "butt" and the visual pun of the framing speakers and a person's behind, sits together with a seemingly old-fashioned aura and the use of undoubted craftsmanship.

CREATE BERLIN

DESIGN *Martin Christel, Codeluxe*

CREATE BERLIN presents itself as "an initiative by and for Berlin designers," working to promote their work around the world. An open competition was held to design a logo for the organization, with figures such as Erik Spiekermann and Carl Frech forming a jury to choose the winner. Many of the 100 or so submissions took the conventional approach of deriving a logo from a well-known feature of Berlin, such as the Brandenburg Gate. The winning design by Martin Christel, however, took a much more radical approach. "The logo is punched manually," he explains. "It 'injures,' it marks, it makes use of coincidences. It has no particular color, its specific character is caused by the creative processes of others too. In an abstract form it shows the initials of CREATE BERLIN."

THOU SHALT NOT MAKE A LOGO OUT OF PUNCTURED HOLES ... AND HOW TO BREAK IT!
Swap the branding iron for a hole puncher, and show you're serious about creative ingenuity.

✝

FEEDBACK
"The 'embossed label' is radical and it almost hurts just to look at it. That suits Berlin, that suits a city that in so many ways comes across as torn, punctured, and edgy."

PROFESSOR CARL FRECH, JURY MEMBER

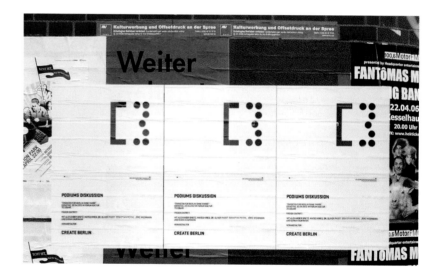

DIANA KAUFMANN
GESCHÄFTSFÜHRUNG

CREATE BERLIN E.V.
IM POSTFUHRAMT BERLIN
AUGUSTSTRASSE 5A
D-10117 BERLIN

FON +49 30 28 09 28 08
FAX +49 30 28 09 47 12
MANN@CREATE-BERLIN.DE

DESIGNATED AREA FOR LOGO MARKING
VALID ONLY WHEN PUNCHED OR STAMPED

DESIGNATED AREA FOR LOGO MARKING
VALID ONLY WHEN PUNCHED OR STAMPED   **CREATE BERLIN**

LEE & DAN SPECIAL PROJECTS

DESIGN *Design Friendship*

THOU SHALT CREATE A LOGO AND NOT AN ARCHITECTURAL MODEL

... AND HOW TO BREAK IT!

If you want to convince your clients that you really are different, a conventional logo won't do.

Lee & Dan Special Projects is a creative agency based in London specializing in creating viral campaigns and the like. It briefed Design Friendship to develop a brand identity and stationery that would reflect the humorous, bold, and experimental nature of its work. Rather than a conventional logo, what evolved is really an architectural visualization of the company's name. "The visual identity developed into their very own research building where they can carry out their 'special projects,'" is how Natasha Shah at Design Friendship describes it, adding, "the letterheads had a graphic net of the building on the reverse, so that Lee and Dan enthusiasts could make their very own Lee and Dan headquarters." As the brand colors are fluorescent, all the stationery was screen printed to get a high-quality finish and to make sure that the colors were as vibrant as possible.

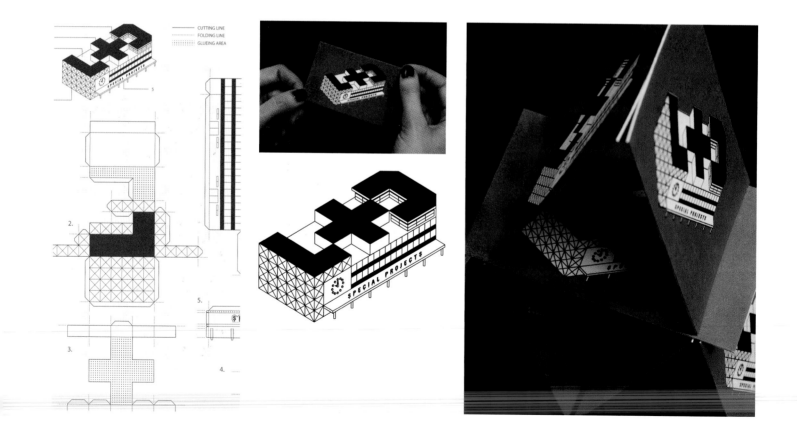

PRETTY GREEN

DESIGN *Design Friendship*

**THOU SHALT NOT HAVE A BUTTON
BADGE IN THINE LOGO
... AND HOW TO BREAK IT!**
Adding buttons that people can detach
and wear makes the identity more
memorable and interactive.

Pretty Green is a self-styled "brand incubator and brand communications agency." It asked Design Friendship to develop an identity that would be "cool, contemporary, clean, and represent its friendly and welcoming approach to all projects and clients." The basic logo is very simple and designed to be as friendly as possible, but is also designed in such a way that the basic motif of a circle on the cloud can be reinterpreted as an additional layer, either purely visually or by becoming a superimposed button badge. "There is no set way of using it," explain the designers. "This versatility adds a tactile element to the logo, whether it is a [button] badge on a thank you card or the overprinting on the business cards."

Cloud9

DESIGN *Dave Sedgwick*

This logo was created for a party balloon company; they wanted something that was instantly recognizable and easy to remember. Taking his inspiration from TV weather reports and the expression "to be on cloud nine," Dave Sedgwick drew up a simple humorous logo where less is certainly more. "You read the symbol/numeral combination as cloud9 without the need to actually put it into words," he explains.

THOU SHALT SPELL OUT THE COMPANY NAME, NOT CREATE A PUN
... AND HOW TO BREAK IT!
Logos don't need to be serious, especially for a company such as this: and when a visual puzzle is so easily decipherable, who needs words?

✝

F E E D B A C K
"Of all the logos I've ever designed, this one gets the most reaction; it's earned me lots more jobs."
DAVE SEDGWICK

SAUSAGE & MASH CAFE

ART DIRECTION AND ILLUSTRATION
Vic Polkinghorne, Sell, Sell!
DESIGN *Judith Wilding,*
Delicious Industries

THOU SHALT NOT CREATE

SEXUAL INNUENDO

... AND HOW TO BREAK IT!

Grab people's attention with the
joke and convince them that you're
unpretentious and worth a try.

A new chain of eateries, the Sausage & Mash Cafes, wanted an identity that would be distinctive and look "established" yet be unpretentious, to match the food on offer. The final result was a light-hearted design in which a series of little characters were mixed with the double entendre of the S&M abbreviation of the company's name. "The overall feel is warm, comfortable, and friendly. The characters add some 1950s-style charm and leave no doubt in the mind of the passerby as to what they sell, regardless of nationality," says Judith Wilding who worked on the design with illustrator Vic Polkinghorne. "We explored numerous directions including a more corporate-style route, but felt it was too impersonal for this brand." Rather than a single logo, the result was an organic assemblage of elements and characters that could be adapted for different applications.

✝

FEEDBACK
"The identity was very well received and proved very versatile–the characters are a definite favorite with the customers."

SERPICO

DESIGN *Eirik Seu Stokkmo,*
Scandinavian Design Group

Serpico

THOU SHALT MAKE THE LOGO PERFECT

... AND HOW TO BREAK IT!

Looking like melted mozzarella, the
logo avoids seeming too new and slick.

"Serpico is a pizzeria in Oslo making pizza the traditional Italian way in a
stone oven and with good ingredients. But it isn't a posh place, and these
aspects needed to be reflected in the logo," says Eirik Seu Stokkmo. If
pizza restaurants are places where a romanticized image of Italy fights with
the reality of bad lighting, paper tablecloths, and tasty pizza, they do not
tend on the whole to think much about their logos, which often are as
old as the interiors of the restaurants themselves. So rather than create a
slick logo, Stokkmo decided to "capture this spirit of imperfection" with a
hand-drawn logo, so as to emulate classic, older logos. "Modern redesigns
tend to aim for perfection and slickness, doing away with the crudity of
older logos. In a sense, this logo holds on to the look of logos that haven't
yet been redesigned," says Stokkmo.

CHEEKY MONKEY THEATER

DESIGN *Nod Young, Khaki Creative*

THOU SHALT NOT BE A COPY CAT

... AND HOW TO BREAK IT!

Referencing people's existing relationship with a famous logo is different to a mere rehashing of it.

Cheeky Monkey is a small, irreverent theater company based in Beijing, which wanted an image of a cute monkey to describe the curious nature of its project. *I Heart Beijing* was Cheeky Monkey's first play, a comedy describing the cultural collision between East and West. The logos for the theater and the play had to work for both local and foreign audiences. A very traditional Chinese folk artform, the paper cut, was referenced for the main Cheeky Monkey logo. For the play, cheeky recourse was made to one of the most famous of all logos—Milton Glaser's I Love New York. "For the great majority of people around the world, this logo is very well known and is recognized as the symbol of a city," says Nod Young at Khaki Creative, which is also based in Beijing. "I decided to use Chinese calligraphy to freshen up this design and to help [local people] to develop a closer relationship with the I Heart Beijing logo. At the same time, I wanted to keep the English 'I' to symbolize the exchange and fusion of Chinese and foreign cultures."

THE FADERS

ART DIRECTION *Paul West and Paula Benson*
DESIGN *Paul West, Nick Hard, and Andy Harvey*
Form

The Faders were a girl punk-pop band signed to Polydor, which released two successful singles before disbanding. London-based design agency Form won a pitch to design the visuals for the band, coming up with a scratched logo inspired by the distinctive linear graffiti that is often seen etched into the windows of buses and trains. An accompanying icon featured a skull that on closer examination shows itself to be made out of musical instruments.

THOU SHALT NOT DEFACE PUBLIC TRANSPORT

... AND HOW TO BREAK IT!

Jog people's memories and get their attention with an unexpected take on something they have seen many times before in a different context.

THE MODERN

ART DIRECTION *Paul West*
DESIGN *Paul West, Andy Harvey,
and Claire Warner*
Form

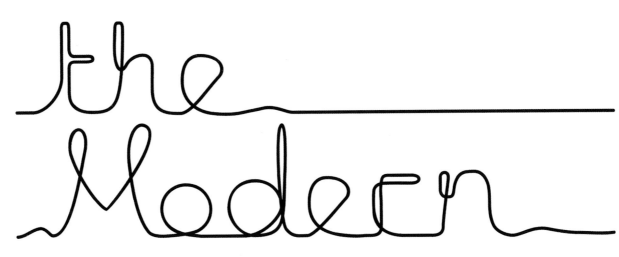

**THOU SHALT NOT CREATE A LOGO
FROM BENT WIRE
... AND HOW TO BREAK IT!**
By making the viewer wonder if
the logo is made from string, wire,
or neon, the mark becomes a piece of
graphic furniture with a life seemingly
of its own.

Mixing 1980s electro pop with burlesque cabaret, The Modern are "musical magpies," say graphic design studio Form, which was asked to create an identity and packaging for the band. "The typography on the 'Jane Falls Down' cover took its inspiration from a set of old metal phototypesetting plates we have in the studio," the designers explain. "To enhance the idea of eclectic 'found' collage materials, we designed a 'Modern' postage stamp and created rubber stamps which change with each release, but which remain central to the identity of the campaign. The logo is a vector version of the original that we created from bent wire."

✝

FEEDBACK
*"The artwork mirrored the band perfectly and
was quirky, yet pop with nods to the past."*
HANNAH NEAVES, PRODUCT MANAGER, MERCURY RECORDS

Featured Designers

344 Design
www.344design.com

999 Design
www.999design.com

Accept & Proceed
www.acceptandproceed.com

Airside
www.airside.co.uk

Alter...
www.alter.com.au

Base Design
www.basedesign.com

Bastardgraphics
www.bastardgraphics.com

B&Co
www.bnco.com.au

Become
www.become.se

biz-R
www.biz-r.co.uk

Boy Bastiaens
www.stormhand.com

Blackbooks
www.blackbookstencils.com

Chris Bolton
www.chrisbolton.org

The Brand Union
www.thebrandunion.com

Bunch Design
www.bunchdesign.com

CHK Design
www.chkdesign.com

Codeluxe
www.codeluxe.com

COLLINS
www.collins1.com

Anton Corbijn
www.corbijn.co.uk

David Barath Design
www.davidbarath.com

Delicious Industries
www.deliciousindustries.com

Design Friendship
www.designfriendship.com

Design Is Play
www.designisplay.com

Die Transformer
www.stazerdesign.de

EMMI
www.emmi.co.uk

Erretres Diseño
www.erretres.com

Espionage
www.thinkespionage.com

Experimental Jetset
www.experimentaljetset.nl

Fluid Design
www.fluidesign.co.uk

Form
www.form.uk.com

Glitschka Studios
www.glitschka.com

Grafiksense
www.grafiksense.net

Hjärta Smärta
www.hjartasmarta.se

Diego Hurtado de Mendoza
www.diegohurtadodemendoza.com

IE Design Consultancy
www.iedesign.co.uk

Apirat Infahsaeng
www.syntheticautomatic.com

Dušan Jelesijević
www.dusanjelesijevic.com

Jordangate
www.jordangate.co.uk

Max Kaplun
www.maxkaplun.com

Khaki Creative
www.khakicreative.com

Kursiv
www.kursiv.dk

L&CO Design
www.l-and-co.com

Index

Acknowledgments

I am deeply appreciative of the many talented designers from around the world who took the time to share and discuss their logo designs with me and bravely shared feedback on their work. As always, working with everyone at RotoVision has been a pleasure, and I would particularly like to say a big thank you to Liz Farrelly for her suggestions and guidance at the start of the project and to my editor Jane Roe for allowing things to run so smoothly. Thanks too to Morris and Winrow for coming up with a design that is so in the spirit of the book.